# My Highland Perthshire
## A Nature Notebook

LAVINIA GRANT

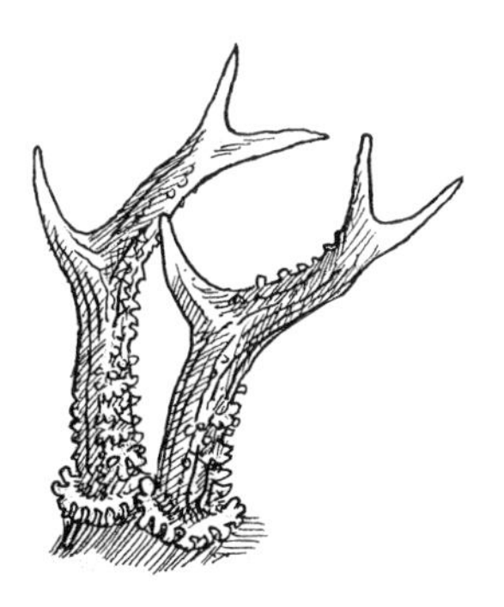

*Roe horns*

*To my Mother*

Published in Great Britain in 2007 by
Watermill Books
The Watermill
Mill Street, Aberfeldy
Perthshire PH15 2BG
www.aberfeldywatermill.com



British Library Cataloguing-in-Publication Data

A catalogue record for this book is available from the British Library

ISBN 978-0-9554358-0-5

Designed and typeset by Lesley Beaney and Janet Dunn, Brora, Sutherland
printed and bound in Singapore under the supervision
of MRM Graphics, Winslow, Buckinghamshire

Published in conjunction with Lavinia Grant

Acknowledgements

My especial thanks to Lesley Beaney and Janet Dunn
for their hard work on typesetting and designing this book,
and for their patience with all my changes and ideas,
as well as to MRM Graphics for their advice and guidance.
Also to Kevin and Jayne Ramage for thinking the book worth
publishing, and going ahead with it.
Thanks also to the local landowners for not shooting me on sight,
and to my family for allowing me space to write the book.
Last, but not least, to my Mother
for her constant encouragement always.

Front and back endpaper illustration *Lime sp.*

# Contents


Introduction 5

Opposite the Hill 7

Winter 35

Spring 67

The Forest 99

Summer 131

Changes 163

Autumn 195

## *On a spring evening, from my room*

Milk-baby voices of lambs
Answered by guttural dams
In the field as dusk falls –
Last games of chase
A mistle thrush practices curlew calls
Twenty, thirty times,
Pleased with them after his
Chorale of ravishing notes
Sung from the thuja's peak
Against sky pricked by a star.
Tawny owl whets her voice
Like sharpening a carving knife
From the wood.
Around the spun coins of
Robins' songs pipistrelles
Scoot on the evening air
Hunting ephemeral insect throngs.
From the hazels, a pheasant's rusty yell
As bat-flighted woodcocks ply
To their boggy corner by the Holy Well.
Now lambs are quiet
Last noisy blackbird's gone to bed.
A passing car breaks the spell.

# Introduction

In 1965 my family came to live beside Loch Tay opposite Drummond Hill in Highland Perthshire, surely among the loveliest places on Earth.

For four years I lived at Portbane Cottage with my parents and developed the habit of writing illustrated nature notebooks and doing paintings and drawings of the wild animals and plants of the area. It was a way of being immersed in the beauty of the place and collecting together an impression of the rich variety of wildlife to be found here; and this activity also helped me come to terms with the recent death of my brother, James.

In 1970, Guy Grant, a Kenyan rancher whose family came originally from Inverness-shire, and I, were married by the Reverend Kenneth MacVicar in the Kirk at Kenmore. Guy and I then returned to his ranch in Kenya, but we have continued to visit Portbane where I paint and write up the nature notes from which I have pieced together the written part of this book to go with the paintings; nearly all of which were done life-sized direct from nature although here many have been reduced in size. Some of the place names used are family inventions and do not appear on maps, and the location of a few places is kept secret.

This is a 'Nature Study' in the old-fashioned sense – that thing which is said to make scientists shudder – and I expect there are mistakes and oddities in it and that there are people, more knowledgeable, who could have made a better job of it. But I hope it may give interest and pleasure to those who enjoy the beauty of wild things and places, as I do.

Lavinia Grant
*November 2006*

Sun's flare and moon's shine
On jagged hill and Highland heath,
Chattering burn and heaving loch
Sparkling birch and furry pine –
It matters not who owns the land;
Passion has made it mine.

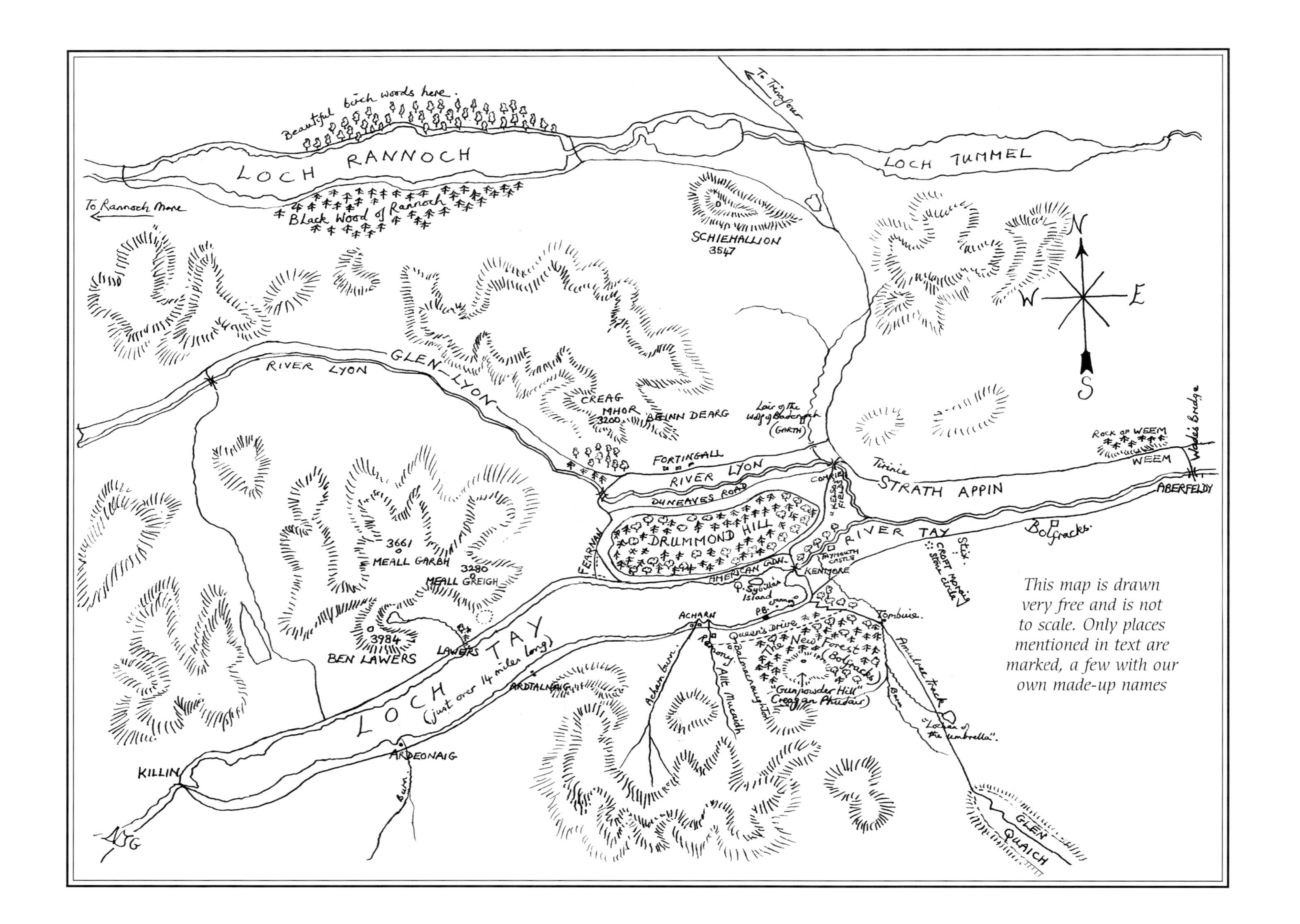

Beautiful birch woods here.
LOCH RANNOCH
To Rannoch Moor
Black Wood of Rannoch
To Trinafour
LOCH TUMMEL
SCHIEHALLION
3547
N
W
E
S
RIVER LYON
GLEN LYON
CREAG MHOR
3200
BEINN DEARG
Lair of the Wolf of Badenoch
(GARTH)
FORTINGALL
RIVER LYON
DUNEAVES ROAD
DRUMMOND HILL
FEARNAN
AMERICAN GDN.
KELSO FIELD
TAYMOUTH CASTLE
KENMORE
Tirinie
STRATH APPIN
ROCK OF WEEM
WEEM
Wade's Bridge
ABERFELDY
RIVER TAY
Bolfracks.
Stix.
CROFT MORAIG Stone circle
This map is drawn very free and is not to scale. Only places mentioned in text are marked, a few with our own made-up names
3661
MEALL GARBH
3280
MEALL GREIGH
3984
BEN LAWERS
LAWERS
LOCH TAY
(just over 14 miles long)
ARDTALNAIG
KILLIN
ARDEONAIG
Burn
ACHARN
Acharn burn
Remony
Balmacnaughton
Allt Mucaidh
Queen's Drive
The New Forest (Bolfracks)
"Gunpowder Hill" Creag an Fhudair
Tombuie.
Amulree track
Burn
"Lochan of the umbrella".
GLEN QUAICH

# Opposite the Hill

Loch Tay lies like a fresh-run salmon between the high hills; its silver flanks freckled with scales of light, brightened or darkened by the sun, the wind and the rain; dimmed to steely grey by wintry skies, or to gunmetal by the equinoctial gales of spring and autumn. At the eastern end of it lies Drummond Hill* – not large as hills go, but with an almost mystical presence which causes it to be for me the point of reference for the surrounding landscape, like a lodestone to some internal compass.

In winter this hill is furred with bare larch trees on the lochward side, umber and shaggy as the pelt of a bear and warm-seeming against the snowy summits and great blue-shadowed corries of the higher hills. In spring when these hills are still pied with ribs of snow, white against their darkness as a dipper's breast is white against his chocolate plumage, a faint tinge of green gradually steals upon the larches; and as the snow continues to melt you notice that, suddenly, they are covered in bright, fresh green. Months later, when some of the heavier greens of summer have begun to pass, a tinge of gold appears here and there as individual trees turn colour until, almost overnight, the whole hill is flaming with the brilliant oranges and yellows of autumn.

The loch itself is constantly changing. Sometimes it is as opaque as pale satin, or glass-smooth with the mountains upside-down in perfect detail upon its surface. On days of gales when the loch is dark and smoking, flattened in great fans by a wind that whistles train-like between the hills, hurrying columns of spindrift tower thirty to a hundred feet into the air, curling and twisting until lost in the larches of Drummond Hill. Then, amber-crested waves crash on the stony beaches and birds struggle to control their flight. Or when there are mild and boisterous winds from the west, the loch turns to navy blue, its surface covered with countless crests of white which come and go.

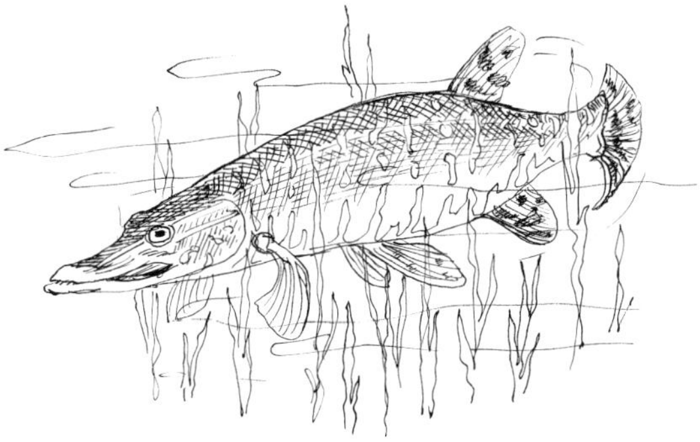

*Pike*

* The name Drummond derives from the Gaelic *druiminn*, locative of *druim* = 'at the ridge' (from *In Famed Breadalbane*)

Salmon parr

On a winter's morning when everything is rimed with frost-dust, the still, dark water steams as if it is boiling; but it is liquid ice. Even in summer the water of the loch is cold enough to make immersed hands ache, except at the shallow end near the village of Kenmore, for it is very deep and, before recent warmer weather conditions, there used often to be snow on the hills every month of the year except in August; and even in August small patches of snow could sometimes still be found in the highest fastnesses. Indeed, the water is still cold enough for Arctic charr, which live in Loch Tay.

Arctic charr

Apart from salmon, brown trout and Arctic charr, there are pike in the loch, said to be favourite prey of ospreys. Pike hang unmoving except for the constant fanning of spotted glassy fins, in weedy bays and inlets, waiting for smaller fish, perhaps a perch, to venture too near. Minnows are found at the mouths of burns and at the outlet of the River Tay. Nowadays there are sometimes escaped rainbow trout from a fish farm, the target of weekend fishermen from Glasgow and elsewhere. When fish farms began we thought them a good idea for they would surely relieve pressure on wild stocks. But disease, to which the unnaturally crowded and confined farmed fish are prone, spreads easily in water and the expected recovery of wild stocks has not occurred. Wild salmon continue to decline and have even stopped returning at all to some salmon rivers in Scotland. Escaped rainbow trout are said to affect badly the native brown trout.

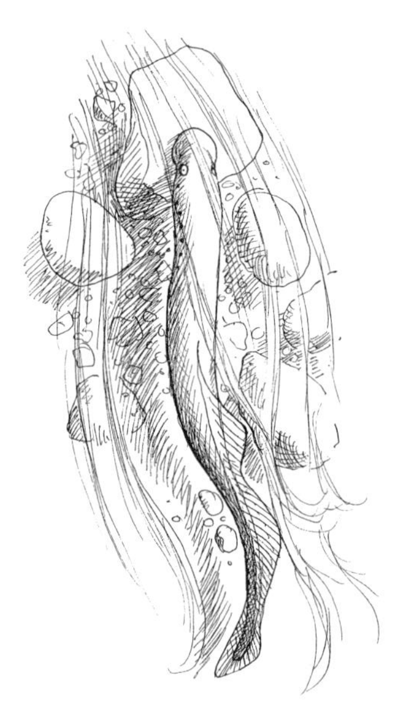

Lamprey

Once our children found a river lamprey attached by its sucker to a stone in the mouth of the Allt Muchaidh (Pig's Burn), or Remony Burn. They and eels must be common but because we do not often spend time looking into the water they are seldom seen. In fact, the loch below its expressive and beautiful surface, as well as being cold, mysterious and dark, is reputed to be haunted by dangerous

*Kenmore Bridge from Drummond Hill. Built 1774*

currents and is more forbidding and inaccessible to most of us than even the high hills in winter storms can be. Without a wet-suit, life expectancy is not very long in this water; and there have been tragedies in Loch Tay to prove it.

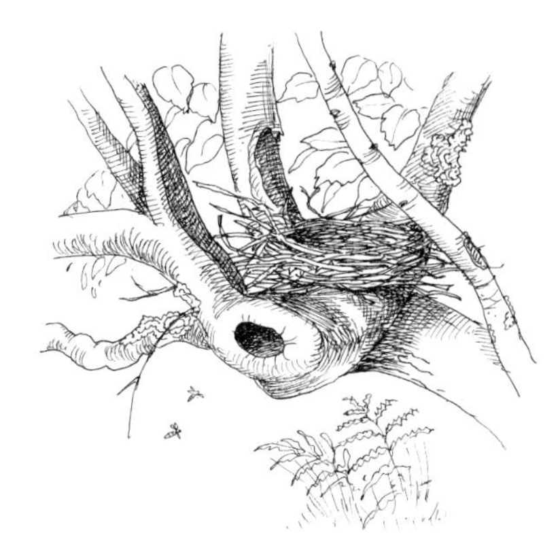

*Old nest of turtle dove. The hole contained a wasps' bike*

From behind Portbane Cottage by the loch, fields slope steeply to a lichen-covered dry-stone wall beyond which are 'the Hazels', an ancient, owl-frequented woodland of previously coppiced hazel, birch, hawthorn and blackthorn in which the children of Kenmore used to hunt for nuts in autumn, and in which I once found a turtle dove's nest. Above this wood the steep slope continues across the Queen's Drive – a scenic track made for the young Queen Victoria to drive along in her carriage when she stayed at Taymouth Castle in 1842 (at which time Lord Breadalbane was keeping some American bison in the grounds of the castle) – through 'Curlew Wood' and up to the crest of 'Gunpowder Hill'*, which we see from our bedroom windows. We have often watched birds of prey – golden eagles, kestrels, buzzards, peregrines, and ospreys (the latter increasingly frequent) – floating about this hill top, or beating to west or east.

*Osprey*

In the fields there used to be a rich growth of ragwort in late summer upon which many black and yellow-striped cinnabar moth caterpillars fed. Ragwort is a pointer to fertile land and is important to many insects. It makes a durable and attractive yellow dye, as my mother discovered when she used it to dye some mohair she had spun that I had brought from our angora goats in Kenya. Although dry ragwort is poisonous to livestock it, and the thistle, aerates the soil. The ragwort, however, was more or less eradicated by the farmer using the fields at that time and with it the cinnabar moths and their caterpillars which are now rare here. The ragwort was replaced by a volunteer crop of meadow, creeping, marsh and slender thistles upon whose tiny, bitter seeds large flocks of goldfinches often came to feed, with greenfinches, chaffinches and siskins. Sometimes thistle-down lay in buff drifts five or six inches deep on the ground. The thistles, too, were eventually much reduced although in some years they reappear. Now nettles are slashed and sprayed though many kinds of butterflies depend upon them and sheep enjoy eating nettle flowers (and thistles) which add variety to their diet. However, the fortunes of such plants wane and wax with the attitudes, prejudices and attentions of farmers and landowners and with weather conditions and grazing.

*Cinnabar caterpillars on ragwort*

Likewise, the man-engineered disease myxomatosis has not exterminated rabbits in the fields although the rabbit population comes and goes locally because of it, so that in some years there is hardly a rabbit to be seen and in others there are many. One year we noticed young rabbits with black scallop-markings on their faces. These we called 'the Zebra clan', while others, with a small white mark between the eyes, were 'the Petal clan'. There have been black rabbits in the

*'Zebra clan' rabbit*

* The proper name of this hill is Creag an Phudair, which may derive from the Gaelic for 'gunpowder', and not from 'fugitive' as is sometimes suggested – hence our family name for it.

*Rabbit*

fields behind the house too, glossy and brown-eyed. We used to grow vegetables in our garden so would try to keep rabbits out although we did not shoot or trap them. Rabbits, of course, are important food for buzzard, eagle, fox, wildcat, badger, otter, stoat, weasel and pine marten, and were good food for people too. As a family we ate and enjoyed wild rabbit when I was a child, after the war and before myxomatosis. In years when rabbits are numerous, predators such as buzzard and fox do well and probably some pressure is taken off the field vole (a predator's staple) which allows them to increase also, which in turn feeds more predators (although the cyclical crashes and peaks in vole population are said to be not only related to predation).

*Resting rabbits*

With so many other creatures keen to eat them one might imagine a rabbit's life to be a constant emergency and the rabbits always on the verge of nervous breakdown. But wild rabbits are able to relax as I discovered when I had crept up on a group that were sitting companionably in the sun in the field behind the house, stretching luxuriously or rolling sideways on the turf. As I lay on my stomach peering over a hummock with only my head showing as I sketched, one young female saw me. Sitting bolt upright she began thumping a hind leg hard on the ground, while her eyes bulged with the importance of her discovery and a piece of vegetation dangled from her mouth, unchewed. To my surprise the other rabbits barely looked up and I was able to continue drawing for some time, then go away quietly without them discovering why their companion had been alarmed. Perhaps that individual had cried 'wolf' too often.

Young rabbits are very playful, cavorting, chasing, jumping over each other and playing 'King of the Castle' – in spite of being the cynosure of every predatory eye. Fear of man in rabbits may be taught rather than inherited, for after a particularly bad die-off of adults from the devilish myxomatosis, surviving young rabbits showed no fear of us even if we ran directly towards them when we were kicking a ball in the fields where these youngsters were feeding. At that time, young rabbits in the garden virtually ignored us. In fact it is often possible to get near to wild rabbits that seem more curious than afraid. The stoat, however, is a different matter.

*Alert rabbit*

Although they certainly fear the stoat inordinately, we have twice seen stoats failing to kill full-grown rabbits. The first occasion was on the road by Portbane.

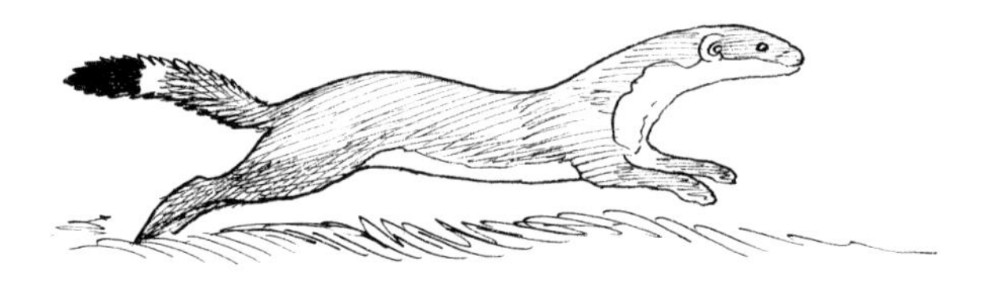

*Dog stoat*

Hearing cries I looked out of my bedroom window to see a full-grown rabbit running down the middle of the road, moving slower and slower until, apparently paralysed with fear, it fell on its side; when the stoat which was following it attacked it. Along came a car! Rabbit and stoat jumped up, the rabbit bouncing round the corner into the lane, the stoat running in the opposite direction like thistledown in a hurricane. The rabbit spent the rest of the day under weeds in the lane, frightened but unhurt. The stoat did not return.

*Hare's 'form' from above as if with 'roof' removed*

The very next day we came upon the second instance of this apparently unreasonable fear in rabbits. Near the Amulree track which leads steeply up the hills to Glenquaich, a large rabbit lay on its side 'allowing' a stoat to bite it although its skin was unbroken. I picked it up and gradually its eyes stopped bulging with terror. Carrying it some way down the hill we released it, apparently having recovered its wits. But on other occasions we have seen stoats and weasels lapping blood from the backs of rabbits' necks where they have been able to tear the skin, and seen them dragging, with little jerks, dead rabbits very much larger than themselves. However, my son, Murray, watched a rabbit at Glen Almond rout a feral cat (which had been stalking it) kicking, biting, and finally chasing it away. So were it not for an element of hypnotic fear that the stoat and weasel inspire in them, perhaps partly from their scent (which to me smells musky with a strong undertone of corned beef), a full-grown rabbit should be, and probably often is, more than a match for a small or medium-sized stoat. Some dog stoats, however, can measure nearly two feet in length. We found a huge stoat run over on the road near Tom na Gru that weighed well over a pound. I wish now we had kept the body to measure and weigh properly, for he must have been unusual. Stoats are normally half that size.

*Winter stoat*

In the Highlands stoats usually turn to ermine in the winter, pure white except for the black tips of their tails, although I have seen chestnut-coated stoats in January. Sometimes they climb into trees, and a white stoat is an arresting sight, in the top of a winter-bared tree, as agile, almost, as a squirrel. One that I saw in the Sma' Glen, ridiculously conspicuous in the absence of snow, seemed like a strange white bird wafting over rocks or like a piece of white plastic blowing in the wind, for it appeared long and somehow boneless.

There are brown hares in the fields behind Portbane, normally peaceful characters who lie for hours in the grass like Trafalgar lions or crouched like molehills which they then closely resemble; or stay hidden in their 'forms' until nearly trodden on. These forms are often worn bare inside, with a few tufts of hare's 'down' to show who lives there, and they fit a hare's body perfectly. I think the hares must have to back in carefully to avoid disarranging surrounding grass tufts (although I have not seen this). But as soon as you 'catch' a hare's solemn orange eye, off it goes. Sometimes they lope high on their long legs like eccentric miniature race horses, or follow one another about, nose to tail, weaving in and out, up and down the

*Brown hare*

*Blue hare (changing coat)*

fields, or among the Hazels, and higher up the hillside in the preserves of the blue, or mountain, hares. Perhaps surprisingly, they also sometimes make use of the open rides in the forest on Drummond Hill.

In winter brown hares feed on parts of the fields usually kept green and free of frost and snow by 'flashes' of oozing water, where occasionally there are also snipe probing for insect life; or a heron.

It is amusing to watch hares wash themselves methodically in the manner of cats, rubbing their faces with licked paws, pulling whiskers or ears downwards, licking each foot carefully, and holding a hind leg high overhead in order to clean under the tail. Hares are clever at using 'dead ground' in order to make off unobserved, and will lower their ears when running along behind a slight rise. I saw a hare part tall grasses with a front foot before pushing through them, having ascertained (as it thought) that the coast was clear.

*Blue hare hiding*

Some of the hares behind Portbane manage to survive shoots which have happened, to my dismay, when a line of men with dogs marches through the fields frightening the sheep and discharging numbers of cartridges out of all proportion to the hares actually killed (once I counted 40 shots although the bag was 'only' seven). Sadly many are caught in snares set for foxes.

Blue or mountain hares, food of eagles, live on the slopes of Gunpowder Hill and on all the high hills around and beyond. In the summer their fur is almost the colour of a purple plum with the blue bloom on it, except for their grey legs and belly and grey, black-tipped ears and all-white tail. But in winter they turn pure white all over. Blue hares have ancestral bunkers – very short burrows about their own length – in banks or under old tree stumps in which they shelter from the eagle's eye or from inclement weather. In hard winters these hares sometimes come down to the fields along the road and we wonder if occasionally the two kinds of hare interbreed (although one reads that they do not) for we have seen a number of puzzling-looking individuals. Some years blue hares are very abundant and in others scarce. One year there were so many that a drab winter field by the roadside became alive with living, bouncing snowballs. Sometimes they are still in their white coats in May.

*Hornet*

One spring, Kelso, my brindled greyhound, surprised a blue hare in the Hazels which made off through the trees when he barked. A few seconds later we saw it bouncing away up the hillside between the rocks. But it behaved strangely, weaving and winding in and out and constantly back-tracking. It seemed to be laying a labyrinthine scent trail – but all the time it was in plain view, conspicuously white against the green hill. Gradually it worked its way back towards the wood and disappeared into it near the place we had first seen it, presumably feeling that it had thrown off any pursuit by its own astuteness.

*Young brown rat*

When we first came to Portbane, the birch trees in the garden across the road below the fields were only a few feet high and blackcocks – 'bubbly-jocks' – came

*Kelso*

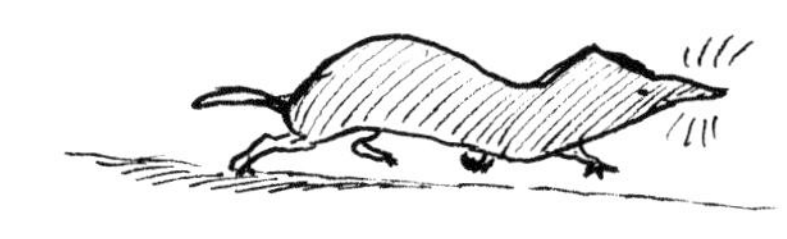

*Pygmy shrew*

to dance among the primroses there; so quiet was the lochside road in that first spring. Black grouse were more common then – perhaps because many fields of oats and barley were still grown along the lochside. Part of that garden was, as it still is, a mature wood and although it stands in less than an acre, for its size the wood contains a surprising number of different kinds of trees – around thirty-one species surviving – for, we were told, it was once a tree nursery for Taymouth Castle. Some of the holly trees must be very old – one has a circumference around its trunk of eight feet; very large for a holly. In the leaf litter there live many invertebrates, and birds forage there during winter. In springtime there are primroses, wild snowdrops (which produce quantities of seed), bluebells, bugle, forget-me-not, and clumps of sanicle which used to be used in the curing of wounds and which indicate the ground is not acid.

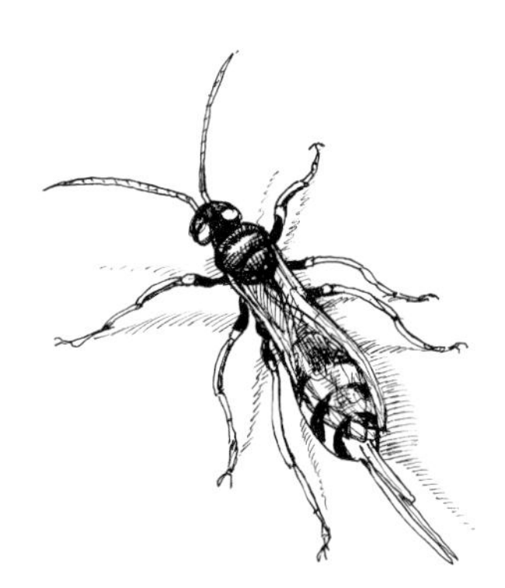

*Wood wasp*

The wood is a staging-post for hunting tawny owls, and heaps of sticks or logs provide cover for the wood-mice and shrews they hunt, breeding grounds for various insects, and hibernacula for hedgehogs. Roe deer, brown hare, blue hare, rabbit, weasel, stoat, mole, wood-mouse, red squirrel, brown rat, vole, shrew and hedgehog have all been seen in that woodland garden. The trees shelter pipistrelle bats and the clouds of flying insects they feed on, and in late summer these bats have a small breeding roost in the roof of our house. They sometimes fly around the tree tops as early as 4pm in summer sunshine. Once I found a dead long-eared bat in the wood. There are moths and many other insects (once a visiting woodwasp or horntail – a huge fly that mimics a wasp – about 3.5 inches long, impressive-looking though harmless) and very occasionally the now rare hornet.

The trees and the hedge along the side of the wood give roost and nest-site to many birds including blackcaps, greenfinches, goldcrests, tits, bullfinches, wood pigeons, and occasionally in the past, stock doves. Pheasants, sometimes wounded, escape the autumn shoots there. Blundering and naïve as the captive-reared ones are to begin with, pheasants very soon learn (after the first shoots) to be frightened of man and become clever at dodging and avoiding him. They fulfil a useful function for other wild animals by warning when people are around, being the noisiest and

*Greenfinch on her nest, in crevice of sycamore*

also among the earlier of reactors. Once I saw a cock pheasant avoid the beaters at a shoot by balancing on a small stone out in the edge of the loch under an overhanging thicket, where he stayed until peace returned. Pheasants often refuse to fly, running zig-zag with heads held low, invisible except for undulations in the grass. Or they creep behind a tussock and lie down, slowly raising their heads like periscopes to keep an eye on the danger. They roost in our wood nearly every night throughout the year, coming in noisily with 'cocking' calls, and talking to each other with subdued croaking sounds. I have heard cock pheasants apparently warning other pheasants (particularly hens) of my presence with low, mellow 'barks' sounding almost like a human voice. And they use this voice as a contact with each other. In the dusky light before dawn each pheasant leaves its roost with a brief squeaky whirr of wings, to land heavily on the ground and begin the morning's forage.

*Balancing for rosehips*

Red squirrels build their spherical winter and breeding dreys in the wood. One of these dreys blew out of its tree and I found it as springy as a football (and about the same size), thickly lined with soft, chewed bark and wrapped around the outside with twigs and sprays of the thuja tree in which it had been built. It must have been impervious to cold. The young squirrels look like russet autumn leaves blowing across the lawn that abuts the trees – a lawn consisting mostly of moss, decorated in summer with daisy, buttercup and self-heal, which is often patterned by varicose-vein-like mole-runs just beneath its surface. Thirty-four years ago we brought a tiny larch seedling from Drummond Hill where it would have been crushed on the edge of a track, and planted it in the garden. It is now some sixty feet tall and provides seed for squirrels and siskins throughout the year. It still has the crooked tip which distinguished it in seedling-hood. Dead branches in the woodland are prospected by greater spotted woodpeckers for grubs, and they 'drum' there each spring. But one woodpecker has discovered that the metal cap on an electricity pole near the house makes a satisfyingly loud sound, and that the note varies interestingly according to where it is hammered.

*Squirrels passing*

*Baby red squirrel*

*Cross-section of red squirrel's drey. They push in through the 'wall' anywhere*

Whilst the fruits, nuts and cones of the woodland trees provide feed for birds and mammals alike, the tallest trees are used as song-posts by storm-cock, song thrush and starling: the starlings producing perfect imitations of oyster-catcher and curlew long before the real ones have started to bubble and trill over the hills and fields behind the wood in spring. We have also heard Portbane starlings imitate perfectly blackbird, thrush, gull, kestrel and telephone bell. A blackbird also incorporated 'telephone bells' into its song which we thought surprising, for a blackbird's song is normally conservative though very beautiful.

*Woodpecker drumming on roof of electricity pole*

Jackdaws, rooks and jays come to the wood for acorns and I wondered how they ate these, until one day I watched a rook taking acorns from an old oak near the potting shed (since cut down). Having transferred the plucked acorn to its foot, it held it firmly against the branch with its toes. Twisting blows of its closed beak prised off the skin, after which the kernel was swallowed whole. Jays might well be called 'oak planters' for they are the main agent in the spreading of young oak trees about the country. Newly picked acorns are carried off by them and buried everywhere. Only fresh acorns germinate, and only jays are planting these regularly. Were it not for sheep and people there would be jay-planted oak woods on all suitable hillsides, as there were in the past. Some of these wonderful woods still survive by the loch and the remnants of others, buried in conifer plantations, could be revived if action was taken at once to restore them, as is being done in some other places by the Woodland Trust.

*Greater spotted woodpecker looking for caterpillars*

Sparrowhawks use the cover of our little wood for their ambuscades, whilst the trees often help their intended victims to escape. There is a corner where we have quite often come upon a sparrowhawk plucking its unfortunate prey, sometimes, alas, while it is still alive. A selection of fungi, lichens and mosses are found among the trees and last but not least, small boys come to collect 'conkers' in the autumn – although this game seems to have been mostly replaced by electronic ones. In fact, this wood is of value to a wider assortment of wild things than I can list or even know about. It is really of inestimable value for, of course, it takes a wood many, many years to mature. It seems to me that the chance of seeing wild creatures and hearing bird-song is even more important than the services provided by amenities of the kind that so often replace such remnant, wild

*Sparrowhawk*

*Jay about to bury acorn*

patches – patches that are like storage jars of vital ingredients, waiting only for a little encouragement to spread abroad the yeasty leaven of living things they contain.

*Pied flycatcher*

On the lochward side of the house, alder, ash, birch, sycamore, goat willow, bird cherry and briar provide hunting grounds for siskin, wren, tree-creeper, starling, long-tailed tit and willow warbler. Some years pied flycatchers visit in spring and summer when we hear the cock bird singing day in, day out, from the tallest ash tree. On the rocky foreshore and among the lochside trees before there were jet skis to disturb them (and perhaps soon jet skis will be removed from the loch altogether) mallard, merganzer, sandpiper, oyster-catcher, woodcock and common gull all reared young, as some of them still manage to do. Dippers and grey wagtails ply the water's edge for mayflies and caddis grubs, the searching dippers sometimes moving stones in the water that weigh much more than themselves. The dipper is an interesting little bird, as this entry from an early notebook illustrates:

*Dipper 'swimming' with wings, on surface*

> 28th October 1967: Watched four dippers on the River Lyon where it runs beside the Kelso fields. They nearly always dipped their beaks, as if drinking, before diving in. One stood on a stone singing a wheezing, fluting and 'chipping' song that sounded like pebbles knocking musically together in the stream. The singer blinked continuously, showing white eyelids. Indeed all the dippers were blinking. Today they were not bothering to bob up and down, imitating wavelets, as they often do, but were remarkably conspicuous and solid-looking on their stones and stranded logs. Two swam and dived abreast of each other in water out of their depth. Sometimes they let the current carry them downstream while they floated high on the surface like miniature guillemots, while at other times they had only their heads and tails above the surface, apparently swimming with their submerged wings, for they then kept stationary and were not swept down with the current. Sometimes the dippers made short dives in quick succession, lasting four or five seconds, always resurfacing at about the same spot or slightly further upstream. I was surprised to see that they did very little preening once returned to their perches; just a quick rubbing of their shoulders. When the dippers came to the surface the water rolled from them in pearly drops and their feathers seemed quite dry.

*Mayfly*

Sometimes dippers fly directly out of the water from beneath the surface, or into it from the air. They take a while to get up speed before flying off fast and low along a river or loch shore, making sharp, 'watch-winding' calls as they go.

*Merganzer*

Cormorant, goldeneye, goosander, and merganzer fish below our house, whilst herons come to catch eels on the point where the globe-flowers grow. Herons always seem half starved, too light in flight, as they rock fore and aft with each wingbeat. The ghostly forms of the goldeneyes can be seen moving about quickly just below the surface when they dive, but merganzers use a different technique for fishing. Swimming along with only their beaks and eyes below the surface, turning sharply into the little bays until prey is sighted, they then dive together with a quick porpoise roll. Another technique of theirs is to fly along in line abreast, noisily beating the water with their wings and feet, before alighting and looking quickly below the surface; then flying for another few yards, looking, and flying again. These techniques are used by family parties of about seven or eight birds. At other times they hunt in pairs or alone. Cormorants usually swim fast and deep when fishing, covering distance, surfacing now and again to look around when they are sometimes mobbed by gulls. They can stay below for many minutes.

*Cormorant*

*Merganzers' fishing technique*

*Pair of herons*

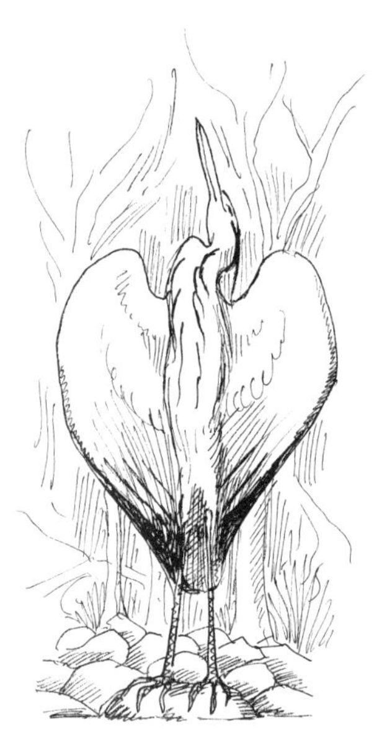
*Heron sunbathing*

In the part of Portbane garden immediately above the loch live typical garden birds such as blackcaps and garden warblers (among the most gifted of singers), spotted flycatchers, hedge sparrows, robins and chaffinches. Very occasionally we hear the fishing-reel songs of grasshopper warblers. In 1997 I saw an eyebrowed thrush, and in two separate years we thought we saw rosey pastors, but did not have good enough views to be certain. My mother saw a small bird she could not identify at the time, which answered to the description of a bluethroat. Never being sure what you might see next is part of the excitement of living here. But even the commonest birds are a delight to watch – for instance the robin which stays up in the evening so much later than most other birds, with its flight soft as a falling leaf or sleight of hand, and its strange swaying displays of aggression. The robin is used to the gloom of great forests where once he was the companion of wild boars and foraged where they turned the loam and leaf litter with their snouts. Now a gardener is 'boar-substitute' for the robin.

On the roof of the house itself pied wagtails sometimes nest whilst wrens, spotted flycatchers and tits make use of creepers and nest boxes on its walls and treecreepers nest in the ridge of the potting shed roof. In the spring of 2000 we put up man-made martin and swallow nests, and that year swallows and house martins built their own nests and reared families under the eaves for the first time since we had lived at Portbane, bringing the mud for building from the fields behind. To our joy they returned in 2001 and each year since, surrounding the house with their chittering songs in spring and summer. We wonder why they did not nest here before.

*Pied wagtail with begging young*

*House martins*

*Gunpowder Hill from my bedroom window. Portbane*

*The edge of Portbane wood*

*Winter on Loch Tay, Nov. '96*

*Three rooks over Drummond Hill from bathroom window, Oct. '98*

May 2001

*Clutch of pheasant eggs (Portbane garden)*

*Feathers from cock ring-necked pheasant*

Dec. '98

*Goldfinches on blackthorn, Dec. '98*

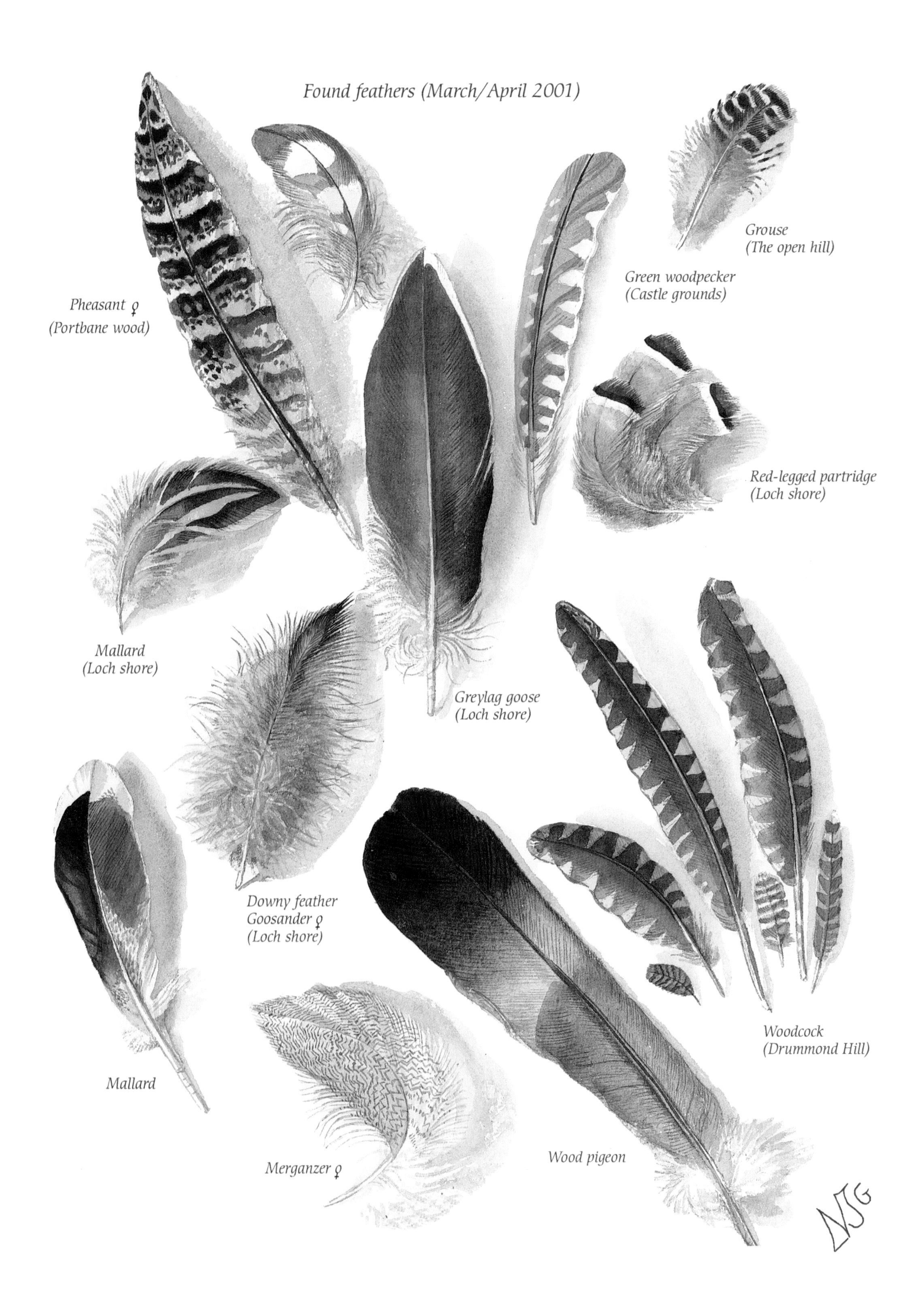
Found feathers (March/April 2001)
Pheasant ♀
(Portbane wood)
Grouse
(The open hill)
Green woodpecker
(Castle grounds)
Red-legged partridge
(Loch shore)
Mallard
(Loch shore)
Greylag goose
(Loch shore)
Downy feather
Goosander ♀
(Loch shore)
Woodcock
(Drummond Hill)
Mallard
Merganzer ♀
Wood pigeon
NJG

Small tortoiseshell
Common field, or creeping thistle
(Cirsium arvense)
Sept. 2002
Seed heads
Aug. 2002
Sept. 2002
Creeping thistle
stunted specimen
NJG

Flowering Plants, Oct. '98
Red Campion
(Melandrium rubrum)
Ragwort
(Senecio jacobaea)
Red Admiral
Yarrow
(Achillea millefolium)
NJG

*Sprig of unusual variety of lime with seed, from below.*

*A very old lime tree (fields behind Portbane)*

# Fungi

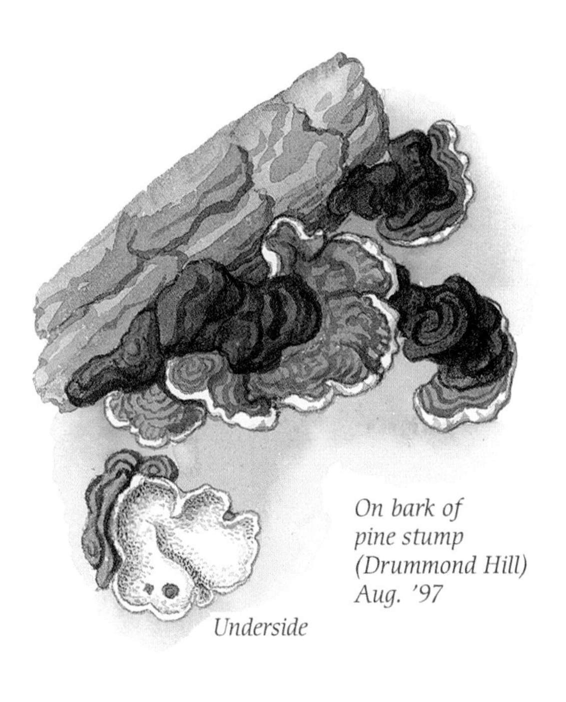

On bark of
pine stump
(Drummond Hill)
Aug. '97

Underside

On stump
under firs
(Drummond Hill)
Aug. '97

Geastrum triplex
(Portbane woodland)
Sept. '97

On stump of
deciduous tree
Nov. '98

Lycoperdon
perlatum
Oct. '98

In the American woodland

*Sketches made on Remony*
*late May 2003*
*Blue hare*
*(Lepus timidus scoticus)*

*Brown hares from memory sketches*
*Portbane fields*

Sketches of Dippers by Loch Tay and the River Lyon (Cinclus cinclus)
whirring upstream . . .
. . . bobbing on stones . . .
. . . swimming on the surface . . .
. . . moving heavy stones in order to find . . .
. . . caddis grubs

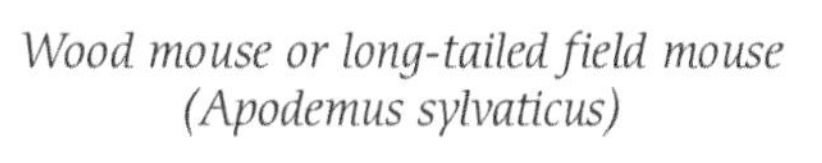

*Wood mouse or long-tailed field mouse*
*(Apodemus sylvaticus)*

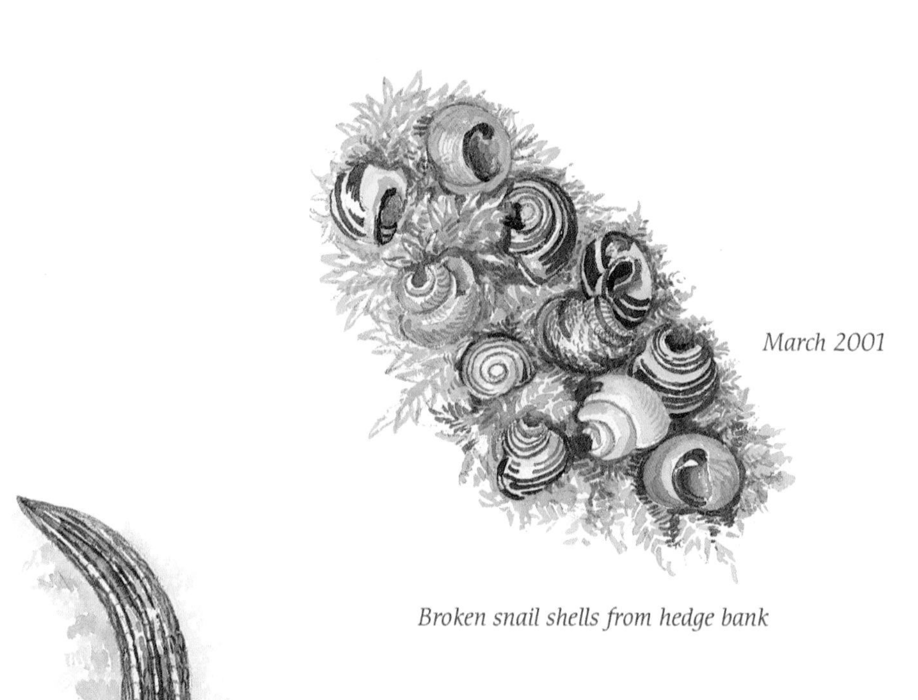

*March 2001*

*Broken snail shells from hedge bank*

*Leopard slug (Limax maximus)*
*(often very large)*

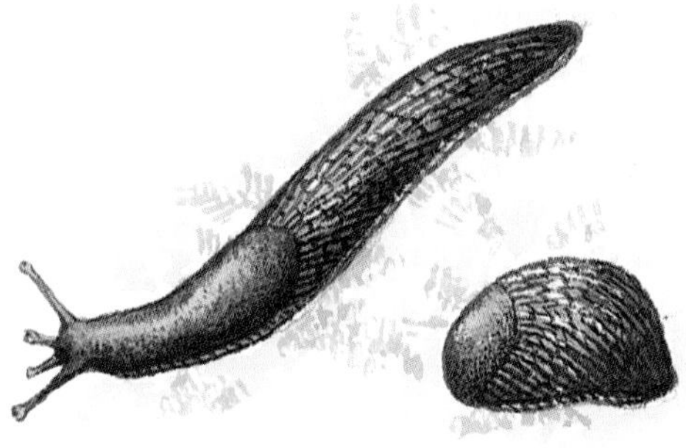

*Arion ater*
*(often very large)*

Aug. '97
Stinkhorn (Phallus impudicus)
young specimen
This fungus emits a pungent, putrid stench
which attracts flies and wasps

# Winter months

November
Trickle of robin's song like melancholy squeezed from a heart.

December
Kirk and snow, fire and song; nights dark and long.

January
Shivery as a violin string, frost-fresh as face washed in icy bucket.

February
New catkins yellow over last year's sodden bracken.
A woodcock lands like a falling leaf.

March
Coltsfoot flowers on a beach of stones.
Tumbling ravens in a fast, bold sky.

*Robin on willowherb*

*The Kirk of Kenmore seen from Portbane.*
*Built 1579 - tower and transepts added around 1759.*

# Winter

Though one thinks of a year in Britain as divided into four seasons there are really, of course, no clear divisions between one season and the next. Even before winter has begun, with its surgeon's knife of cold, its power to invigorate or destroy, there are signs of coming spring. As fruits and seeds are ripening in autumn new catkins are already tiny on the birch twigs, crimson on the alders, and green on the hazels. As the leaves in autumn fall, the new buds on the tips of the twigs of all the trees can be seen, ready to burst in spring. So although winter is sometimes thought of as the end of the year and a temporary death of nature, it is really a time of gestation out of which, with the energy of the returning sun and lengthening days, spring is fledged. So winter can be seen just as well as the beginning of a year as the end; and each month is as beautiful and relevant in its own way as any other; although it takes time to learn to love November as much as May: November with its melancholy trickles of robin song and the white beard curling on the brown bones of willow-herb; when the dried leaves are deserting the trees in droves like rats leaving sinking ships and on a still day you can hear tapping and rattling all around as they encounter bare twigs on their journeys to the ground. However, over thirty different kinds of wild plants can still be found in flower in November, although they are few and far between.

*Goldeneye - winter visitor*

Some flowers that may be found in November:

Buttercup (*Ranunculus spp*)
Dame's violet (*Hesperis matronalis*)
Climbing corydalis (*Ceratocarpus claviculata*)
Red campion (*Silene dioica*)
Wild pansy (*Viola tricola*)
Field pansy (*Viola arvensis*)
Herb Robert (*Geraneum robertianum*)
Red clover (*Trifolium pratense*)

Climbing corydalis

Gorse (*Ulex europaeus*)
Broom (*Cytisus scorparius*)
Blackberry (*Rubus fruticosus*)
Wild angelica (*Angelica sylvestris*)
Forget-me-not (*Myasotis spp*)
Foxglove (*Digitalis purpurea*)
Cross-leaved heather (*Erica tetralix*)
Red dead-nettle (*Lamium purpureum*)
Harebell (*Campanulata rotundifolia*)
Ragwort (*Senecio jacobaea*)
Scentless mayweed (*Tripleurosperma inodorum*)
Pineapple weed (*Matricaria diccoidea*)
Yarrow (*Achillea millefolium*)
Spear thistle (*Cirsium vulgare*)
Knapweed (*Centaurea nigra*)
Hawkweed (*Hieracium spp*)
Dandelion (*Taraxacum officinale*)
Daisy (*Bellis perennis*)
Nipplewort (*Lapsana communis*)
Groundsel (*Senecio vulgaris*)

Woodcocks from the Continent are returning to the woods in November and December, as brown as the dead leaves; and on bracing days of blue and windy sky, ravens are already starting their courtship, playing in pairs on the up-draughts about the summit of Gunpowder Hill, reaffirming their pair bonds for their very early spring breeding.

November is a good month in which to see ravens from Portbane although they start to play in September. Once there were as many as fourteen together over the hill and, because I often attract their attention by using a rather poor

*Raven*

imitation of their 'cronk' and 'pruuk' calls, I believe they may recognise *me*; although it is difficult to recognise individual ravens, blue-black as they all are. Because they well know I will not harm them it is easy to watch at close hand when they toss sticks to each other, or dive and roll in the sky. When climbing Gunpowder Hill on my own they often continue playing and cruise low over my head. If I call, a raven will hesitate even when seeming to be on its way to somewhere specific (perhaps crossing to Drummond Hill) and will often turn round and come back to look down at me, making a few small circles before resuming its journey. Perhaps this has something to do with an old hunting partnership between ravens and people.

Konrad Lorenz, the pioneer animal behaviourist, wrote that the ravens he reared and which later lived free but kept in contact with him, were among the most intelligent animals he had known. Potentially their life-span is almost as long as our own, so they should have time in which to accumulate wisdom. But

*Crow trap*

*Must be visited every day – by law.*

*Must contain water at all times – by law.*

*Must have sheltered perches.*

*All birds that are not crows must be released at once – including ravens (which are protected by law).*

*The raven is about 25" long, whereas the crow is only 18" long.*

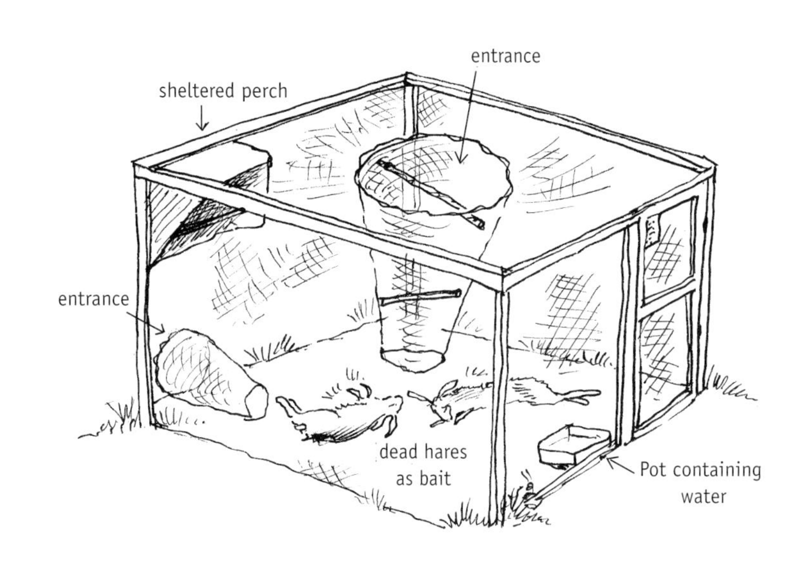

*Raven in portable 'cage' used to decoy others to poison bait. Poison baiting is illegal and ravens are protected by law.*

*Merganzer family fishing technique*

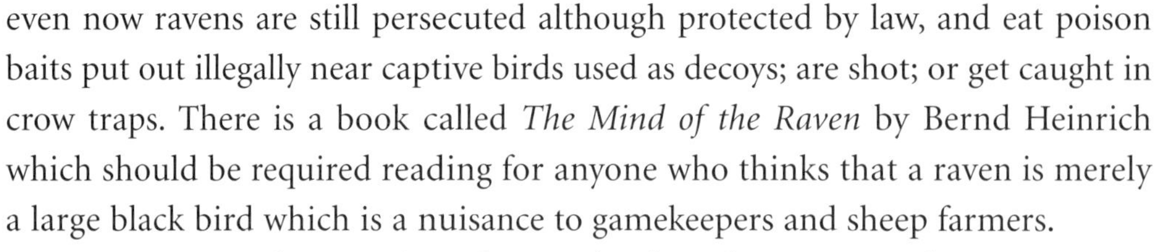

even now ravens are still persecuted although protected by law, and eat poison baits put out illegally near captive birds used as decoys; are shot; or get caught in crow traps. There is a book called *The Mind of the Raven* by Bernd Heinrich which should be required reading for anyone who thinks that a raven is merely a large black bird which is a nuisance to gamekeepers and sheep farmers.

*Snow goose*

On raw November evenings thousands of greylag geese used to come tumbling and side-slipping onto the loch, filling the air with that most thrilling of wild music. In November 1967 a boy repeatedly tried to row out to them with a gun, but the geese kept out of range. Now that geese are generally better protected in Scotland, they spend more time at the coast and on the fields and it seems that fewer come to the loch for safety at night – although many still do. Sometimes they come in at mid-day to rest on the water, when they appear pink in the wintry sunshine. It is the greylags that normally visit Loch Tay but one October I saw a snow goose, a wanderer from America, flying up the loch alone. Small skeins of Canada geese now also appear sometimes..

In the winter months, flotillas of hundreds of mallards and rafts of noisy common and black-headed gulls also come to rest on the loch, and small herds of whooper swans float like royal barges on the water. One night of hard frost, swans passed over the house in the dark, their calls in flight thrilling as silver trumpets,

*Treecreeper 'right' way up*

*Treecreeper hopping under branch?*

*Whooper swans*

no longer the deep honking of the birds at rest on water. Just before take-off their voices do become more musical, like the 'low baying of hounds' mentioned in books – much deeper than the voices of the geese.

When winter trees are bare it is easier to see smaller birds too; perhaps a tree-creeper, its little striped cape ruffled by the wind, going up a tree in fits and starts – up, up, up, up it goes, then drops like a stone to a lower branch. Then up, up, up until it drops again, to repeat this manœuvre over and over, sometimes levering off flakes of bark or lichen with sideways twists of its curved bill as it goes and peeping into cracks and crannies, until it has exhausted the possibilities of that tree for small insects and moves to the next. The stone-like dropping of the tree-creeper saves not only time but also energy. It appears to be able to hop along the undersides of branches as easily as on top, but this may be an optical illusion. The little bird's white front is so clean that it looks like an animated snowdrop as it goes about its work in winter. In spring they nest under the peak of the potting-shed roof in our garden.

*Crossbill*

Siskins used to be quite scarce here, but since the post-war creation of forest plantations they have steadily increased. In the winter months they gather in flocks of several hundred and whirl and stream through the trees of Drummond Hill and along the loch shore with tinkling calls, as if gold bells and charms are being jangled sharply together. They swarm into the tops of alder and birch to ransack them for seed and then fly off again *en masse*. As a flock turns in unison all the bright yellow panels in their delicate 'fish' tails jump into view simultaneously.

Cross-bills, too, gather in winter on Drummond Hill, and bound in fast-flighted flocks, sharp-voiced, to the crowns of larches and pines to twist the seeds from the cones with their special, crooked beaks. The rust-red and carmine cocks and plump green hens look like small parrots as they turn about among the tree tops. Once, on the far side of the hill, we saw a two-barred crossbill, a rare vagrant from the east of Europe, or Russia.

*Two-barred crossbill*

One morning so cold that upon coming out of the house it felt as if one's face had been plunged into a bucket of ice-water and every twig was rimed with fluffy crystals of hoar-frost, a pack of snow buntings came flying buoyantly along the roadside by Portbane; the only time we have seen them so low off the hills here, although one thinks of them as wintery birds – and they are indeed birds of the Arctic tundra which find the high hills of Scotland to their liking. They sometimes spend the winter at the coasts.

Although from Portbane there used often to be snow to be seen on the mountains, particularly on Ben Lawers, all through the year except in August (less often in recent years), the first snow to fall at lower levels in winter is always magical. It is preceded by a preoccupied stillness, the sky a blank, lilac-tinted grey against which the snowy hills appear startlingly white. The first random flakes seem accidental, almost apologetic, like migrating butterflies that have lost their way. But soon the air is thick with them and a tiny prickling hiss can just be heard as many millions of flakes touch twigs and ground and dead leaves all around. Once I saw a bullfinch cock experimentally eating a snowflake, as one might eat a small, delicate biscuit.

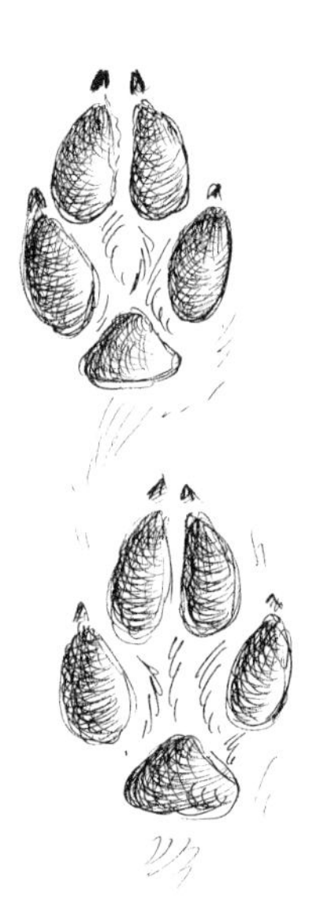

*Fox tracks*

The day after such a snowfall, in a transfigured and silently-muffled world, there may be the tracks of a fox above the hazel wood behind Portbane, strung in a single line, one narrow footprint immediately in front of the other; and a stain of yellow where he has urinated on a snow-covered tussock, to show where he has been and where he is going. I always hope that a gamekeeper will not pass that way and see the signs, for I want foxes to be there as much as he (it seems) does not. In winter and early spring we occasionally hear the skirling of a vixen, or repeated breathy barks, either from The Hazels or from Drummond Hill, and feel happy that foxes exist in spite of the intense persecution that they suffer in Scotland. Indeed, research shows that the constant killing of foxes, by digging,

*Young dog fox*

*Fox in heather*

hunting, shooting, trapping, snaring, gassing and poisoning (the latter two methods now illegal) may be pointless in the case of the fox as it stimulates breeding and young foxes constantly move into unoccupied territories. It has been shown, again by research, that if foxes are left alone their population is self regulating and does not increase after stabilising itself. When we first came to Portbane, drives for foxes were still held when many were killed in one day, and a bounty of 15/- per fox's brush was advertised in the Kenmore Post Office. Once, when on our way home from Perth, we saw the body of a gigantic red dog fox hung upon a gate. He looked easily big enough to have been killing adult sheep, but again, studies have shown that foxes seldom kill even lambs, the percentage lost to foxes each year being very small; although many thousands of lambs die of sickness, neglect, starvation and accidents every year on the hills and in the fields. But the fox has always been a convenient scapegoat. Foxes are happy to eat carrion, and there is seldom a shortage of sheep carrion on the hills, and afterbirths in the lambing season.

*Golden eagle*

Another hunter may come lower down the hillsides in winter. One afternoon as I climbed Gunpowder Hill with Kelso, a foot or more of snow creaking at every step and an icy wind burning from the north west, something made me turn my head. There was a golden eagle, so dark as to be almost black, sweeping up behind us along a shoulder of the hill, its great wings held still except for minute adjustments to the wind. It passed over our heads not more than fifteen feet above and wore on over the next brow out of sight. I saw the amber eye and the yellow cere of its powerful beak, and heard the loud hiss of air through the spread pinions. Kelso too watched the eagle with interest.

It was against the wintry flanks of Beinn Dearg and Creag Mhor above Findhuie Wood at the lower end of Glen Lyon that my mother and I watched a pair of golden eagles displaying – at least the male displayed while the female

*Displaying eagles*

deigned occasionally to notice him. They were moving black dots to the naked eye but through binoculars became clear, and because their aerobatics were performed against a background of snow and black rocks they seemed even more impressive than on the other occasions we have been lucky enough to watch eagles displaying. While the big female wallowed lazily on air currents above the white hillside, the male, perhaps half a mile away, climbed powerfully upwards. At the zenith of his steepling he folded his wings so that their ends touched his tail and he appeared like a black heart. Then he tipped over and dived. The terrific speed of his diagonal descent could be judged by the way the rocks on the hillside behind him blurred and streamed in the circle of the binoculars' vision. Just as it seemed he must strike the ground below the female and kill himself instantly, he opened his wings a little and perhaps at an even greater speed, threw up into the sky again on the momentum of the descent. Up he shot like a lift in a skyscraper until he was as high as he had been before, all without a wing beat. This stupendous dive he repeated until both birds had disappeared from view up Glen Lyon. We were too far away to hear the cock bird's gulping yelps of excitement which we knew from experience he would be uttering.

*Hazel nuts opened by wood mice*

In winter frosts the grass is covered with fiery sparks from the low sun-light refracted in ice crystals – blue, violet, red, orange, yellow, peacock green and diamond clear. Up in the hazel wood the burn is lined with bulbous icicles encasing twigs and splashed tussocks of bleached grasses. Sometimes icicles hang in rows of crystal sausages, fatter at the bottom than the top, and the water tinkles below them under a casement of strangely patterned ice. The ground being frozen hard and the grass and old leaves crisp as sugar-coated cornflakes, it is impossible to walk quietly. On one such day when I was sitting in the snow with my back against the trunk of an ancient hazel, amongst the shells of nuts opened by wood mice, a greater spotted woodpecker flew past. Soon it returned to tweak peeling bark from branches only a few feet from me. Winter is sometimes a good time for watching wild animals and birds although it often seems empty and bleak and the days are so short and the weather so cold. Winter snow may also reveal, through tracks, the presence of animals one might not have known were there – such as otter, badger and pine martin.

*Red squirrel tracks*

The colours of the landscape in winter are often rich and strong. There is the plum of the bare birch-tops, the silver of their trunks amongst the burnt sienna (in some lights almost ox-blood red) of old bracken; and the winter turf is like faded gold-and-green velvet. The hills, with an icing-sugar sifting of new snow on their dark crests, may stand against a cold blue sky. Or the colours may be ethereal, the whole land hazed with frost, the trees a misty mauve in the hollows and by the pewter water of the loch, and the traceries of the twigs of birches so fine that they appear like smudges of smoke. Even the hills take on a fairy cast and although every detail of them can be seen in the clear, cold air, they seem to have lost their substance and become pure light.

At other times the hills are beset by knifing winds that drive the surface of the snow in billowing waves that whip off cornices like fine white sand, stinging and blinding. Sometimes one can see these wind-driven flurries rising like tendrils of smoke into the sky along the top of the great corrie of Ben Lawers, and from the crests of the other mountains.

*Red grouse. 'Plastic' wattles and white-rimmed 'spectacles'*

In January, when winter is often at its coldest, cock red grouse are already proclaiming territories in suitable patches of heather on the hillsides, 'Go-becking' in their froggy voices from the summit of every little knoll, their fringed vermilion wattles inflated while the white rings around their dark eyes give a comical impression of plastic sun-glass frames. Busily they fly to and fro as if anticipating spring, although there are three more months to go before spring-proper arrives, in spite of some days when a mild wind blows from the west, softening the catkins

*View from Portbane in winter*

*Portbane window west-facing*

and lifting little fans and flurries of spray from the burns, while the land comes alive with the sound and movement of running water from melting ice and snow, or rain.

Occasionally the weather is extreme by Loch Tay. The coldest temperature recorded in the winter of 1985 was –23°C (–9.4°F) which occurred on 27 January not far away (at Braemar in Aberdeenshire) in a period of almost arctic weather. My parents were snowed in at Portbane for ten days. Heating of the house then was by a single open wood fire, a small coal-burning Raeburn range, and a few plug-in electric heaters. The windows were not double-glazed and there was no deep-freeze then in which to store quantities of food. The loch froze far out from the edges but because it is so deep, it did not freeze right over opposite Portbane. Mr Stott of Kenmore remembers an earlier Arctic winter when the loch froze right over and people were curling on the ice by Kenmore. From the warmth of Africa I wondered about my parents and how the wild animals would survive. Many deer, particularly yearlings, died. The stone walls disappeared and fences were buried in snow over their top wires; but the electric fences, of which there were many fewer then, although buried, must have electrified the surrounding snow for, as Mrs A Duncan-Miller of Remony told us, the starving deer would not cross them. Small birds, too, must have found it hard to survive that winter.

On January 15th 1968 there was a hurricane, with wind speeds of 134 mph at Glasgow, the strongest recorded in Britain at that time. The wind which came

*Thujas in the hurricane*

*Portbane Wood after the hurricane*

screaming down Loch Tay from the North-West that night was travelling at about 120 mph and although the stone walls of the house are 2 feet 6 inches thick, Portbane trembled in the strongest gusts. But so stoutly built are the houses of Scotland, and so used its trees to savage gales, that the damage was far less than that which occurred in the famous but less severe hurricane many years later in England. There was a frightening high-pitched, humming whine in the wind that night. The old spruce in the Portbane wood was bent like a drawn bow, although its trunk at the bottom was at least three feet in diameter. A grove of flexible thujas lay horizontal to the ground, then, when the wind lessened momentarily, waved wildly back into view as swirling black silhouettes, only to be flattened again and again. You could actually see the wind streaking past, and the outlines of the hills dimmed at each new gust as if their foundations were shaken. The noise of it was so loud we could hardly hear the crack and crash of falling trees just outside. My father and I spent much of the night at our respective windows, although my mother buried her nose in her pillow, saying it wasn't such a huge wind as all that!

*Mrs. Chook bathing in her drinking water*

Next morning most of the big white poplars in our wood were down. A wood of beech trees above the end of the loch was destroyed, branches and trunks a shattered jumble with jagged yellow ends, as if they had been torn apart by a mad giant. Perhaps these trees had already been weakened by fungus. Strangely, one remained undamaged, and a line of beeches along the end of the loch was also uneffected. Drummond Hill looked the same as usual on the lochward side but on the North side most of the plantation trees were lying higglety-pigglety. Electricity was 'out' everywhere, slates and chimney pots were blown off in the

*Wade's Bridge, Aberfeldy. Built 1733 at a cost of £4,095 5s 10d*

cities and many people were hurt, some even killed. But next morning the birds in our garden behaved as if nothing had happened and as far as we could tell all were 'present and correct' – even 'Mrs Chook', a blackbird who at that time, owing to an injury, could not fly.

In February 1990 there was a flood such as no one then living around Loch Tay had seen before, although other such floods had been recorded long ago. It had been a very wet winter and a deep fall of snow melting quickly, combined with heavy rain and the sodden nature of the hills and all the countryside around, meant that more water entered the loch and River Tay than they could hold. Strath Appin was a sea from Bolfracks to Aberfeldy on one side, and from Tirinie to Weem on the other. The Tay's course was marked out in that expanse of water by a narrow lane of trees which normally stood on its banks, but which now had only their tops above water. The road on the south bank of the loch which goes past Portbane was under water at the Kenmore end, and again, three feet deep, before Acharn; and in other places around the loch. The main road at Weem was also inundated. Wade's bridge at Aberfeldy descended into deep water, the river no longer flowing only under it but around it too. A car was drowned on the far side and from the top of the bridge nothing of the strath could be seen that was not covered by a brown sea, rough with waves.

A wind so strong that it blew the distance setting of my camera off its alignment, piled the water of Loch Tay itself high at its southern end. Because the water was held up by the new obstruction of the boating-centre piers it ate away completely the lower banks of our garden and the slipway for our rowing boat, demolishing the old laundry and 'dry-dock' boat shed, and damaging the heavy wooden boat itself, which wallowed upside down in three feet of ice-cold water on the stone floor until rescued. Many creatures must have perished in that flood.

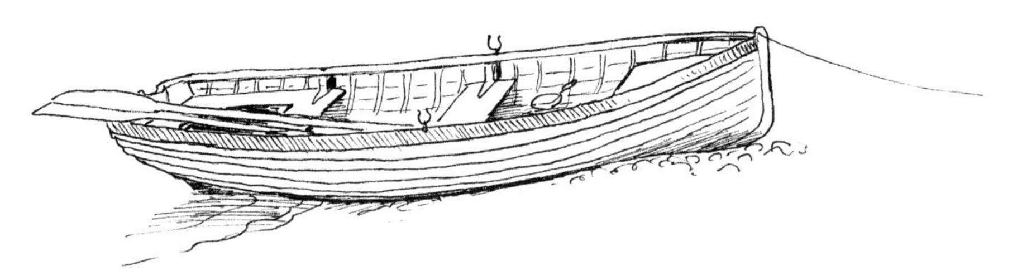

*Portbane rowing boat*

November seed heads
Dock (Rumex)
Rosebay
Willowherb
Broom
pods

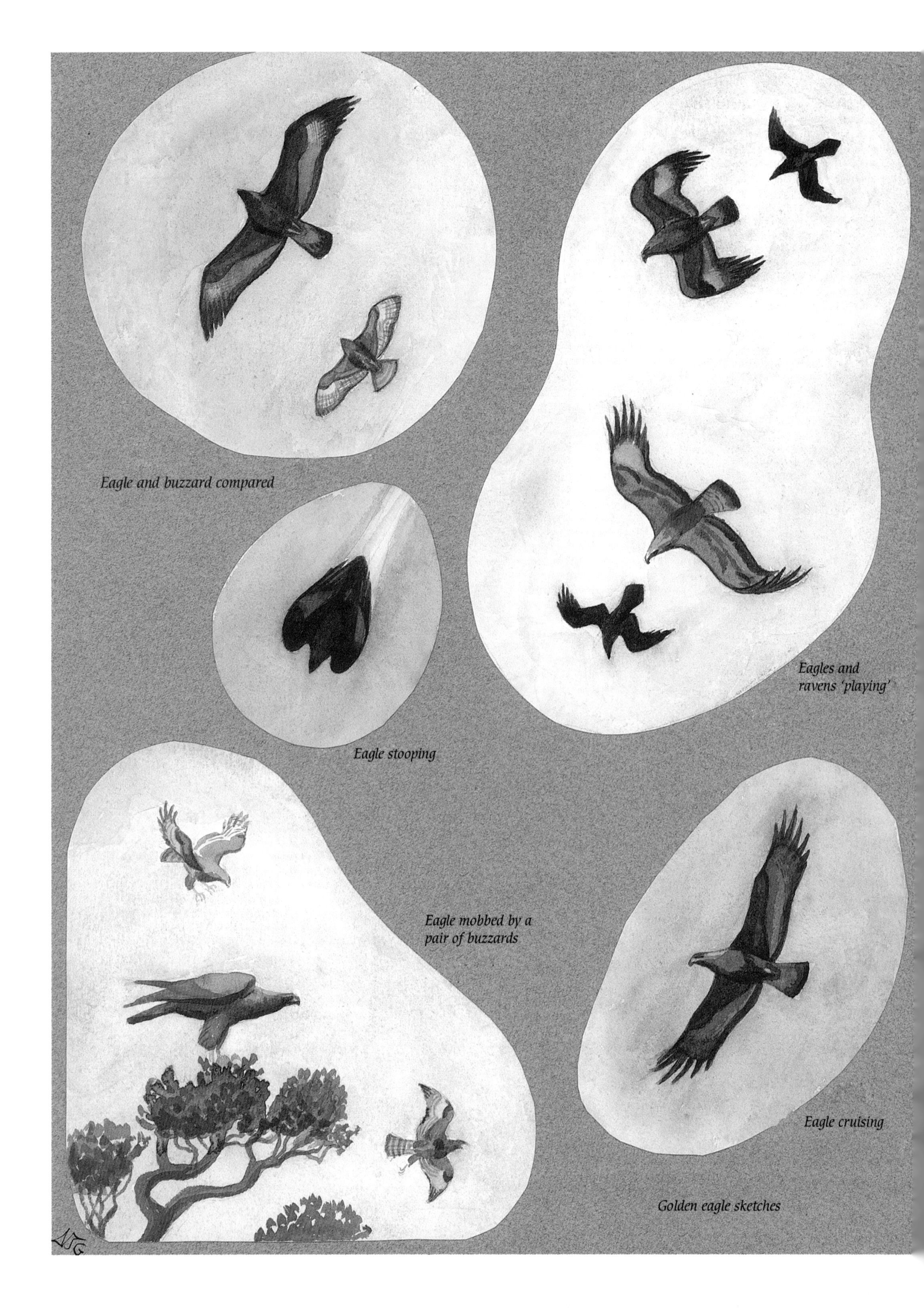


Golden eagle sketches

*Blackcocks and greyhen eating birch catkins, The Hazels, Nov. '78*

*Winter birches towards Loch Rannoch, March 2001*

*Woodcock against background of Drummond Hill, Nov. '98*

*A Roe buck in winter coat and minus his antlers. (Drummond Hill)*

*Snow falling on Drummond Hill, Jan. '90*

*Pair of Goosanders at Strathtay,*
*Jan. '90 (sketch from nature notebook)*

*Looking up Loch Tay to Ben Lawers from Portbane, Feb. 2005*

*The Hazels, March 2006*

*Sketches from memory of Ravens playing in pairs over Gunpowder Hill, Nov. '98*

*Picking up and dropping sticks*

*Hanging on the wind over a stump*

*Schiehallion and the Keep of the Wolf of Badenoch, March 2001*

*Lichens*

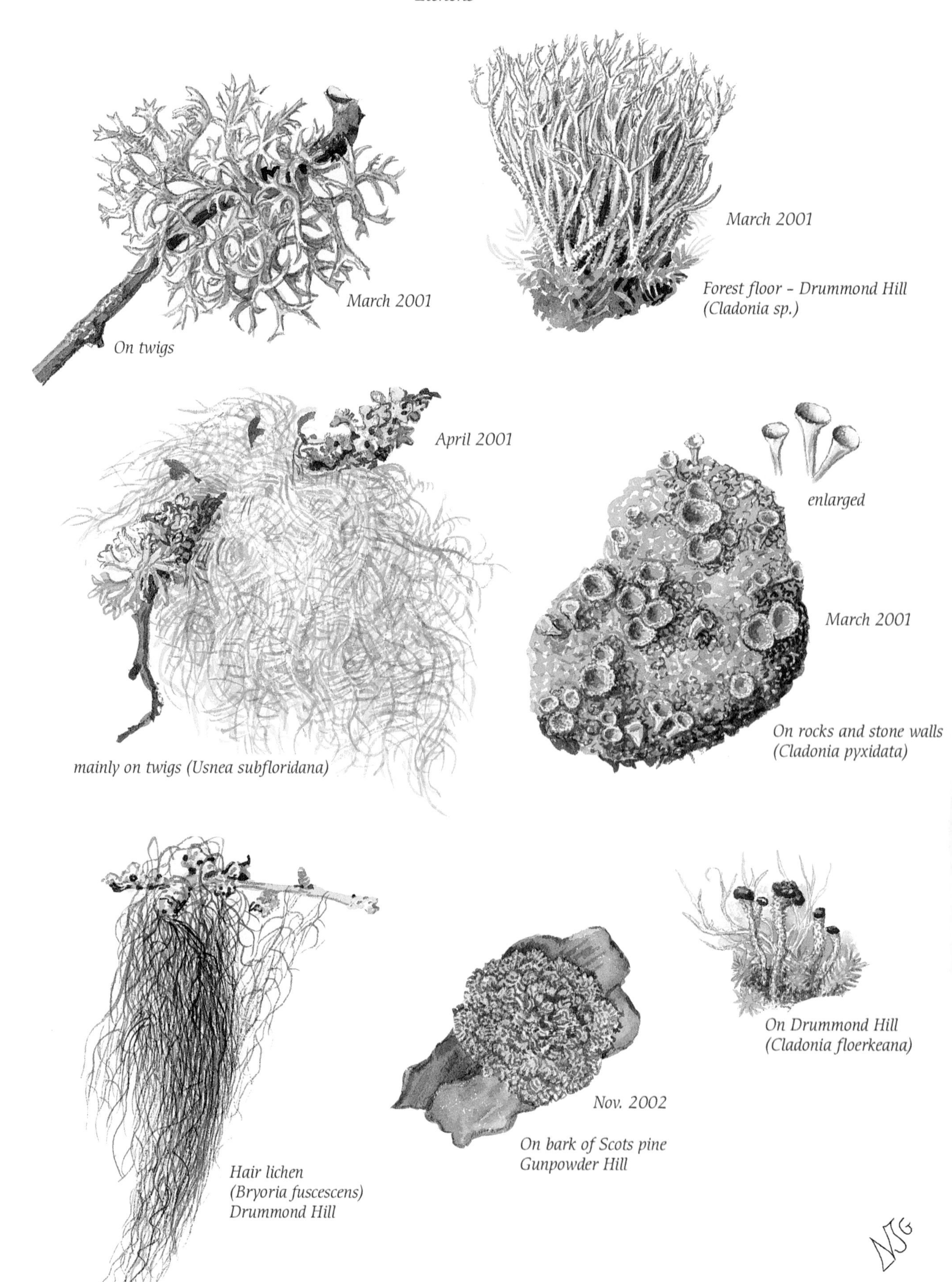
March 2001
On twigs
March 2001
Forest floor – Drummond Hill
(Cladonia sp.)
April 2001
mainly on twigs (Usnea subfloridana)
enlarged
March 2001
On rocks and stone walls
(Cladonia pyxidata)
Hair lichen
(Bryoria fuscescens)
Drummond Hill
Nov. 2002
On bark of Scots pine
Gunpowder Hill
On Drummond Hill
(Cladonia floerkeana)
NJG

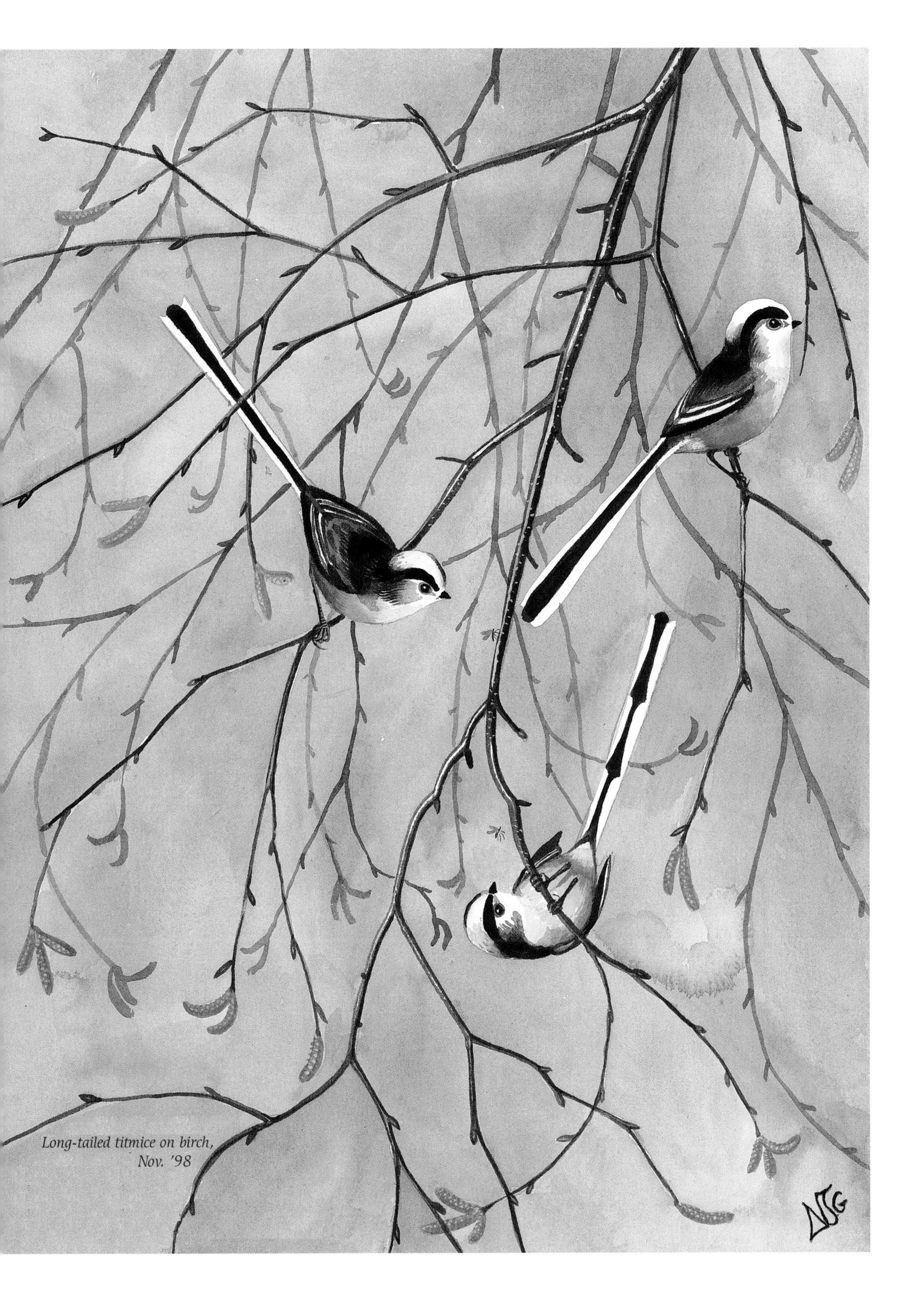


*Long-tailed titmice on birch,*
*Nov. '98*

*Roe does crossing the burn at the top of the waterfall above the Old Manse, Ardtalnaig, Jan. '90*

*Drawn after seeing two Roe deer at dusk, Portbane fields.*
*(In their winter coats)*

*Siskins on Alder, Nov. '98*

Raven
(Found on Drummond Hill)
Heron
(Portbane foreshore)
Buzzard May 2003
(Found in Curlew wood)
Tawny owl
(Found in Portbane wood)

March twigs
March 2001
Hazel
Alder
Pussy Willow (Goat willow)
NJG

# Spring

When Spring comes dancing in green slippers
The hills will still with snow be pied,
No whiter than the breasts of dippers.
Above stars of glossy celandine
And banks of primrose pale and glimmer,
The first fluting curlews cry.

Through hanging hazel-tails yellow
Wavelets grey on lochside shimmer,
And loud-piping oystercatchers ring,
While shy waterfalls of warbler's song
Compose a canticle of Spring.

When tufted larch greens bear-brown hill
And canes of silvered pussy willow,
Twined with emerald-budded leaf,
Make bower for courtship peccadillo
of titmouse, finch and spotted thrush;
Then Spring comes dancing with a will.

*Snowdrops*

*Frog with frogspawn*

# Spring

When winter is nearly over a different-feeling wind, boisterous and playful as a big puppy, ruffles the loch from the west bringing with it a mysterious happiness, as if spring itself is breathing on the world; and the new yellow lambs-tails of the hazel catkins are set astir like the tails of the earliest lambs in the fields. But the coming of spring may vary by as much as two, or even three, months. In early, warm years wild flowers appear in May that are not expected until June, the same applies to some butterflies and moths and to migrant birds. In late, cold years it is the other way, with May flowers not appearing until June and still flowering in July, and migrant birds late to arrive.

*Tadpoles*

Toads and frogs start to breed so early that it is still almost winter (February and March can be the coldest months of all in the Highlands) although they continue to spawn into May. There is a pond tucked under Drummond Hill which is later filled with tadpoles, and there are sometimes newts and big medicinal horse leeches there.

Early, too, brown hares gather to box with their forepaws, to leap over each other and chase madly about the frosty fields in their courtship activities. This happens not only in the traditional month of March but through April into May, and they often play and box at other times of the year.

On shingly shore of loch and river, coltsfoot is one of the first wild flowers to come out, with golden saxifrage along the ditches to be followed later by the glossy yellow stars of lesser celandine, and wood anemones under the alders. On

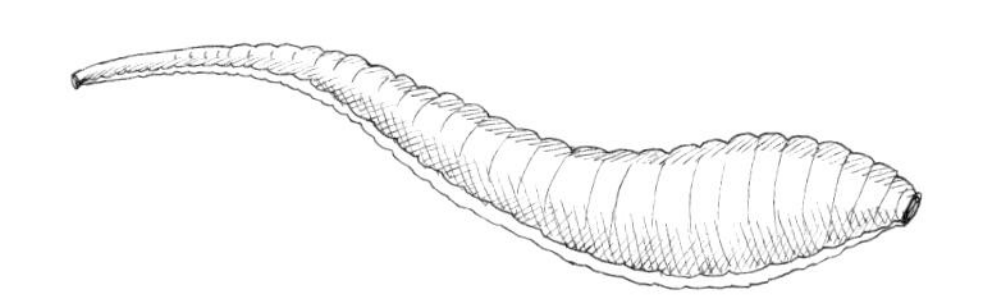

*A large leech*

*Boxing brown hares*

mossy banks cushions of pale primroses appear again, visited by the first slow bumblebee queens that have survived their winter sleep and which search mossy banks and lawns for suitable holes in which to start their breeding nests. Elder is the first tree to put out leaves, like bunches of curly green feathers, although the honeysuckle has had fresh green on it throughout most of the winter. The first blossom, on cherry-plum, damson and blackthorn, is as white as the snow that still sends chill winds across the fields from the hills; the first violets come out along the roadside, and soon fragrant bunches of them cover the sunny places where crooks of bracken will later unfold and the golden curlicues of ferns are already thickly clumped.

*Bumble bee queen*

Birdsong seems to make the spring, and birds themselves dream of singing and practice their songs quietly to themselves, sometimes with their beaks shut. Once I heard a thrush sing loud and clear while carrying a worm in his beak. Sometimes birds sing in flight and the song itself and the individual notes are not affected by this activity. But mostly, birds pour out their songs from perches in their territories. Morning song starts before dawn with the earliest risers: wood pigeons, pheasants, thrushes, robins, blackbirds, hedge sparrows and wrens; while greenfinches, chaffinches, tits and warblers join in later. Each morning with lengthening light the chorus starts earlier and at the height of the spring singing, before nest duties become too exhausting, it begins as early as 3 am.

Early one morning in May 2003 I heard a series of unearthly, wavering shrieks and strange gaggling laughter coming from the misty loch outside my window. It was three black-throated divers displaying to each other, craning their necks to emit these thrilling and incredibly wild calls – sounds which have earned divers the name 'loon' in North America.

Migrant from Africa, willow warblers arrive, unnoticed until the shy waterfalls of their songs begin to trickle through the air on all sides, filling the pauses between the songs of thrushes, the robust bursts of chaffinch song, the trills of greenfinches and the fierce, steam-engine ditties of wrens. Thrushes breed early,

*Black-throated divers displaying*

*Curlew's nest*

*Steam-engine ditties*
*(Wren)*

almost before there are leaves enough to hide their mud-lined nests and cærulean eggs, and the lawn and flower beds in spring are frequented by callow young ones, oddly frog-like as they hop on pale legs, big-eyed, with spotted throats and no tails worth mentioning.

One May I watched a cock pheasant displaying to a pale-coloured hen pheasant in the field behind the house. By puffing up his feathers he had made himself appear twice the size of a normal cock, and whichever side of the hen he found himself (she was walking along looking for food, apparently taking little notice of this magnificent swain) he lowered the wing nearest to her and tilted his fanned tail towards her so that she could not help seeing his splendour. If she looked his way he swelled himself even bigger and shook his tail with little jerks as if to say '*Well*, what about *me* then? *What* about *me*!'

*Displaying cock pheasant*

*The Curlew's semaphore*

Curlews arrive early from Africa and the coasts to whaup and warble from the hill as they sail on uplifted wings in courtship flight. They have a habit of holding their wings over their backs for a second after landing, when the pale undersides show, then closing them with a snap so there is almost a semaphore flash – 'I have landed here'. Their calls when heard nearby begin strangely harsh and tortured, then float up into that lovely mellow fluting so expressive of the lonely hills.

The loud piping of newly arrived oystercatchers resounds over the fields behind the house as they fly together in fast formations or look for places to lay their eggs – perhaps on an old stump, a broken-down wall, or beside a stone in the middle of a ploughed field. Sometimes we see them down by the loch standing with their necks arched so that their orange beaks touch the water, calling 'chee-chick! chee-chick! chee-chick!', while another chants 'chicker-chicker-chicker-chicker!' Every now and again they march forwards together a few paces on magenta-pink legs and repeat their act from the beginning. The winding songs

*Oyster-catcher nesting on stump*

*Oyster-catchers*

*Oyster-catcher display*

and thin piping of sandpipers sound from the shore, too, and between whiles they stamp in the shallows in the manner of flamingos to stir up their food. Common gulls sometimes nest on a rock below the house while on the loch itself ducklings of mallard and merganzer scoot on the surface as if powered by tiny outboard motors. These ducklings and other birds are at risk from tangles of unbreakable nylon fishing line left along the shore by thoughtless fishermen. Each year I collect a sackful of this discarded line between Portbane and Remony Bay alone. Once my daughter Bella and I brought home from Kenmore beach a common gull which we found ensnared and tethered, lying on her back with khaki paddles blowing forlornly in the wind. We nursed her in the bathroom for two weeks, feeding her on sprats and herring bought from the fishmonger in Aberfeldy. Eventually we took her to a rehabilitation centre for seabirds but after an initial improvement she died there – perhaps from delayed shock or infection from wounds made by the nylon line.

*Common gull*

*Mallard with ducklings*

As the first swifts of spring rip through the air on sickle wings, buzzards may be 'scissor-gliding' in courtship flight over the fields behind. Rooks stream past Portbane constantly, on the outgoing journey 'kawing' loud and clear, and upon return their voices muffled by food-filled pouches; carrying provender for their naked, black-skinned nestlings in the trees of Taymouth Castle grounds all day long. They are still passing at 10 pm and fly out again at 4.30 am. A newcomer to the area recently employed a gamekeeper to kill these highly intelligent and mainly beneficial 'agricultural' birds because she did not like the noise they made (and this in their breeding season!) Sadly rooks are not yet fully protected but cannot legally be killed unless they are in the act of 'destroying' crops.

Gean, bird-cherry and hawthorn soon come into bloom, and as spring moves towards summer one of its chief glories appears in deep carpets of scented wild hyacinths under the lightly-leafed trees. And all amongst these bluebells is the

*Sandpipers*

*Buzzard with rabbit*

lacy white of pignut flowers. Hedge-banks are covered with greater stitchwort and aniseed-scented sweet cicely (the young seeds of which are pleasant in salads) and occasionally you may find patches of cowslips. In shady places the white flowers of greater bitter cress, sweet woodruff and wild garlic or ramsons, star the green. Ramsons grows thick in the gorge of the Acharn burn, filling the air with its strong, garlicky smell.

*Youngsters*

At this time the fields are enlivened by the white scuts of baby rabbits flashing on and off like little torches. Later, the buzzards which breed on Drummond Hill ferry rabbit catches across the loch to feed their young, which call loudly from their ragged nest in a larch tree there. Short-eared owls with demanding owlets to feed may be out in the daytime, quartering moorland and rough field. Occasionally a barn owl may be seen, perhaps leaving its roost in an old hazel trunk if you have passed by too close, or hunting The Hazels or Taymouth golf course in the dusk. I once saw one hovering in the bright sunlight of mid-morning, appearing pure white like a huge butterfly.

*Short-eared owls hunting*

*Barn owl in the hazels*

*Cuckoo*

The most evocative sound of spring and early summer is surely the voice of the male cuckoo, sometimes loud and clear, the next minute seeming far away, coming and going like a mellow flute from the folds of the hills. Each cuckoo voice has its own pitch – some alto, some tenor. The females make a different, bubbling call. In the olden days cuckoos were thought to sleep all winter inside special mountains, usually conical in shape: Schiehallion being one of them. Schiehallion can be seen from the hills above Portbane, from the top of Drummond Hill and from the 'Kelso fields' between the junction of the Lyon and Tay, a long slanting ridge leading to the perfect cone of its peak, from where it drops sharply towards Loch Rannoch. Ptarmigan live up there.

Another sound of spring and early summer, less common than it used to be (largely due to the fashion for early-cut silage, instead of later-cut hay crops), are the creaking calls of green plovers, or lapwings – 'pee-wheat, pee-wheat' – as they lap around meadow and hillside, tipping and tumbling on black and white

*Lapwings*

*Lapwings or Green plovers*

*A flock of lapwings*

*Lapwing chick in silhuette*

windmill wings. Sometimes the musical notes of golden plovers can be heard far overhead as a flock passes on its way to breeding grounds in the northern bogs and hills.

*Young lapwing*

---

One April I visited a black grouse leck not far from Portbane. Getting up in the cold and semi-darkness before dawn, I drove a short distance to the bottom of the track which led towards the leck, where I left the car and walked. There was a thick mist that morning through which the ghostly forms of huge larch trees appeared dimly and the rushing of a burn in the ravine to one side of the track could be heard. As I climbed another sound made itself felt, like someone whipping taut wires: an almost electronic emanation. There was an accompaniment of

*Black grouse leck*

rich bubbling that came and went between these 'twangs'. At the place I had been instructed to leave the track I got through a fence, and climbing through grass heavy with dew, came eventually to the edge of an open hillock. Suddenly through the lightening mist the birds appeared. There must have been at least twenty blue-black cocks and many speckled greyhens gathered to watch them. The cocks jumped at each other like Samurai, pirouetted, too-ed and fro-ed, jousting and circling, their lyre-shaped tails fanned to show the targets of their under-tail coverts like white chrysanthemums, their necks inflated and their red wattles spread. Every now and again a female would crouch in front of her chosen cock and they would mate briefly; and all the time those strange and hypnotic sounds resonated through the air. The dance was still going on and it was full daylight when I withdrew and made my way happily homewards. When not disturbed black grouse will sometimes leck for much of the day in spring – and again, less actively, in autumn. In recent years they had seriously declined but may now be recovering with the planting of more natural woodlands. But the leck I visited is no longer used.

*Blackcock*

In May 1968 I found my first woodcock's nest in a patch of bramble, bracken and hazel, only two yards from the road near our house on the lochward side, which is nowadays covered with the concrete quays and buildings of the boating centre. Two birds rose silently almost at my feet. I had seen them a split second

*Woodcock with nest*

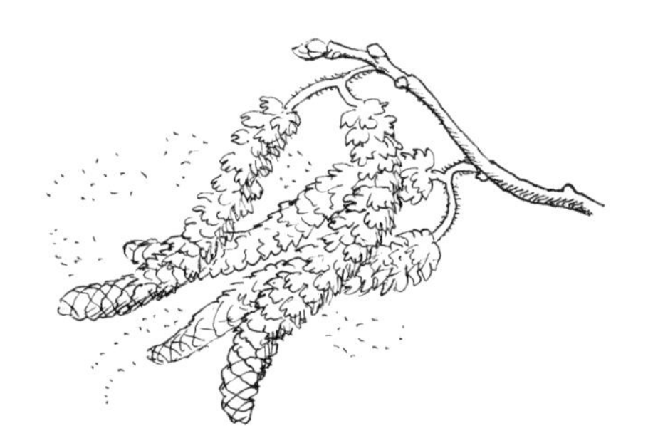

*Hazel catkins*

before and had time to register the soft patterning of their plumage, their large, high-set, dark eyes and long grey bills. After almost hovering for a moment they flitted away; and there was the nest, as deep and perfectly rounded as a breakfast tea cup and tightly lined with brown beech leaves. Inside it were three fawnish eggs with darker mottlings of greenish-brown.

Every evening during April, May and into June, woodcocks would pass along the road in front of our house with their strange bat-like flight, growling, squeaking and whirring in 'rhoding' courtship display – '*prrr-prrr-prrrrr-whis-sawhit*'. They are still doing this although they often fly a different route past Portbane; perhaps there are too many cars for them these days; and I think, fewer woodcocks.

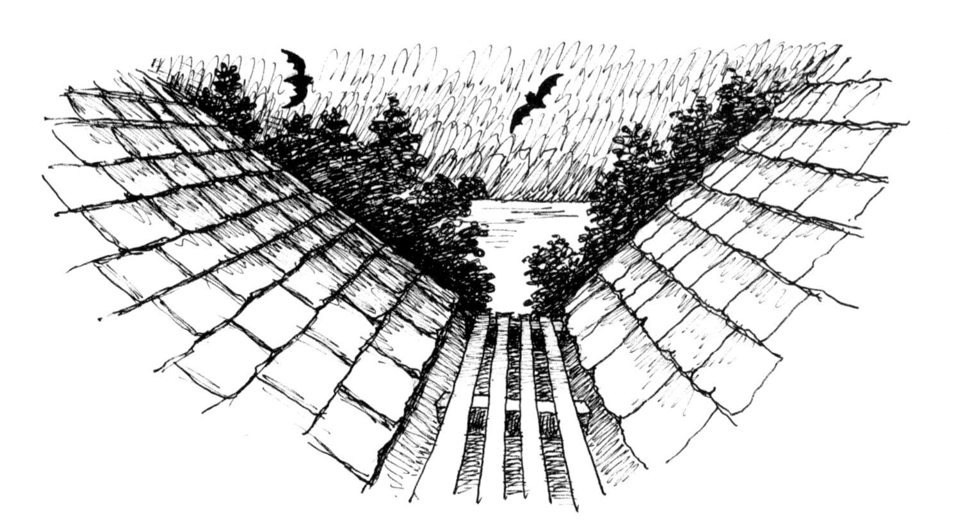

*Pippistrelles over the roof*

It was only four years ago, while looking out of my window each night of that spring visit, that I saw some bats, larger and paler than the earlier-flying pipistrelles, flitting low along the road or flipping over the hedge into the woodland garden. At the same period my daughter, Isabella Nicholson, whilst up with her new baby at all hours in the bathroom that overlooks the loch, noticed the same large bats hawking low over the water; and I have seen them since. We are almost sure these are Daubenton's bats which are particularly associated with woodland near water.

*New lambs*

## Blossom

On the grey apple tree
Fragrant blossom froths free
From winter, cold earth and dead twig;
And garland chains that on the cherry blow
Shed their petals down
As unscheduled springtime snow.
Is all this to please insects
So that apple tree and cherry always grow?
Or has Divine providence
Arranged for that which pleases them
To bring us joy, also?

*Earliest wild flowers*

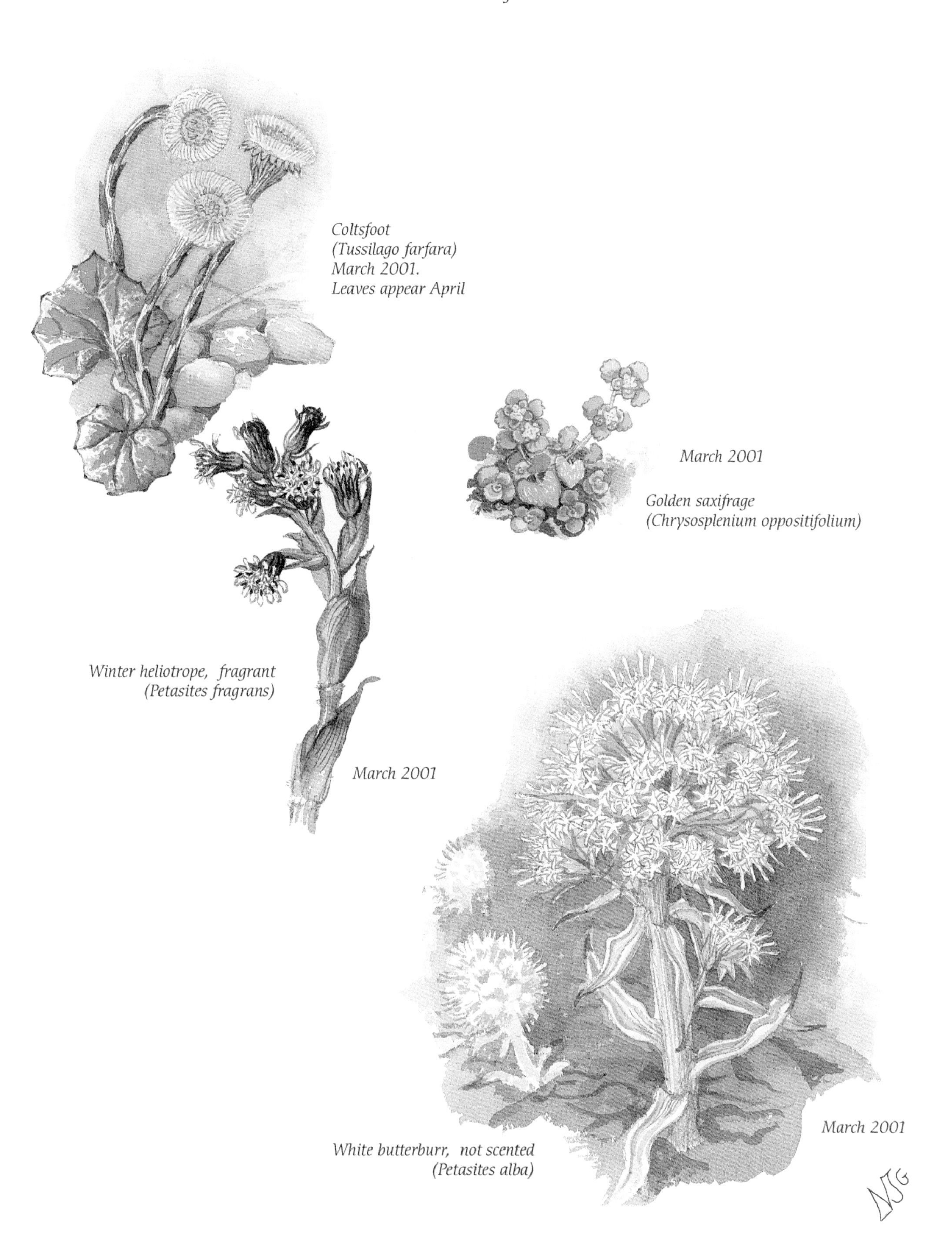

*Cock bullfinch eating prunus buds. Seen through binoculars from bedroom window, Jan. '90. Sketch from notebook*

*Blue titmice on maple. Portbane, Nov. '98*

*Prehistoric standing stones at Tirinie with Greylag geese and Black-headed gulls*

April twigs
Hazel
(Corylus avellana)
Hawthorn
(Crataegus monogyna)
Blackthorn
(Crataegus spinosa)
Bird cherry
(Prunus padus)
Sycamore
(Acer pseudoplatanus)
Goat-willow (Sallow)
(Salix caprea)
April 2000
NJG

*Some flowers of May*

*Ancient Goat willow (In field above Croft-na-Caber)*

# *Ferns*

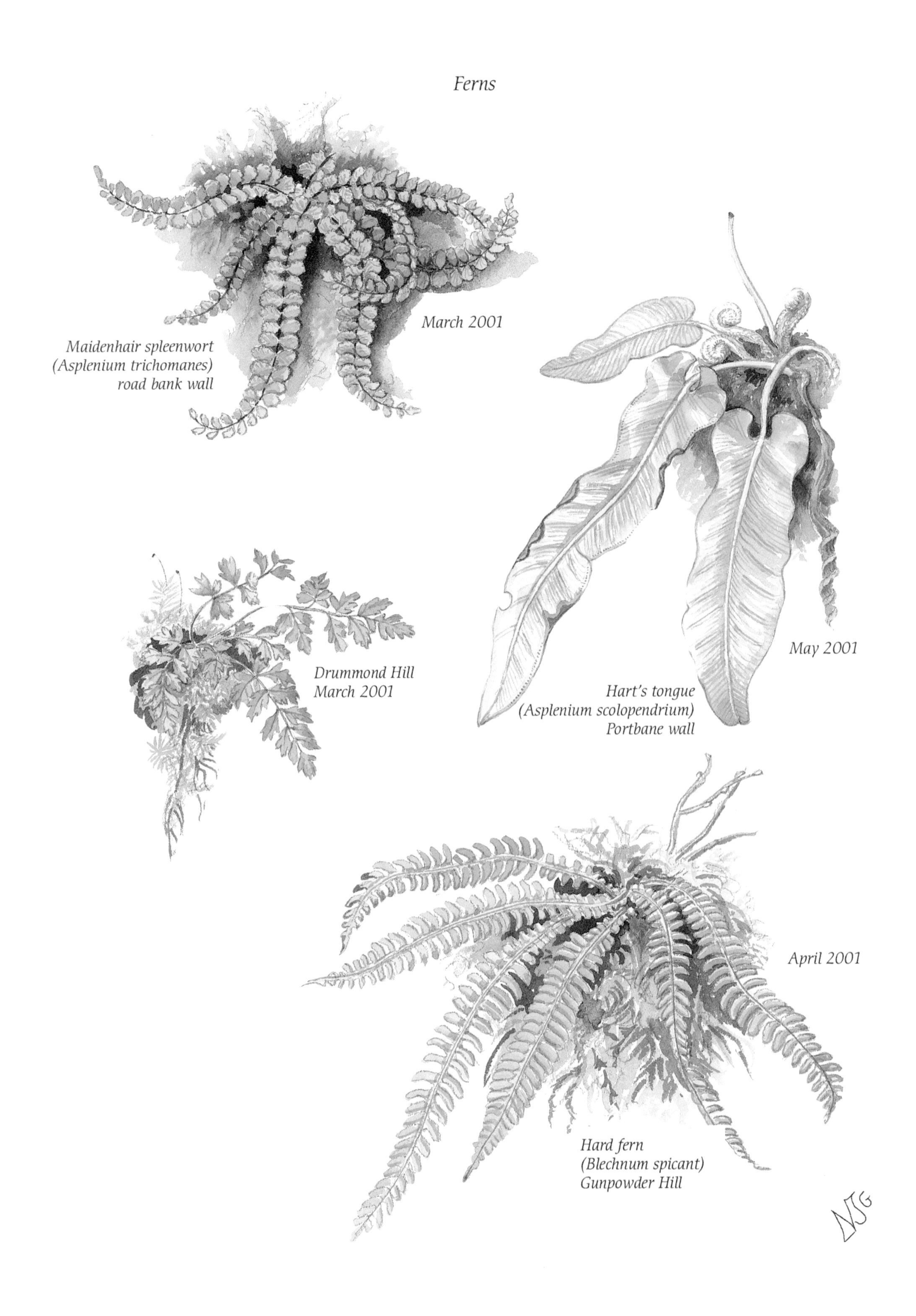
March 2001
Maidenhair spleenwort
(Asplenium trichomanes)
road bank wall
May 2001
Hart's tongue
(Asplenium scolopendrium)
Portbane wall
Drummond Hill
March 2001
April 2001
Hard fern
(Blechnum spicant)
Gunpowder Hill

*Fungi*

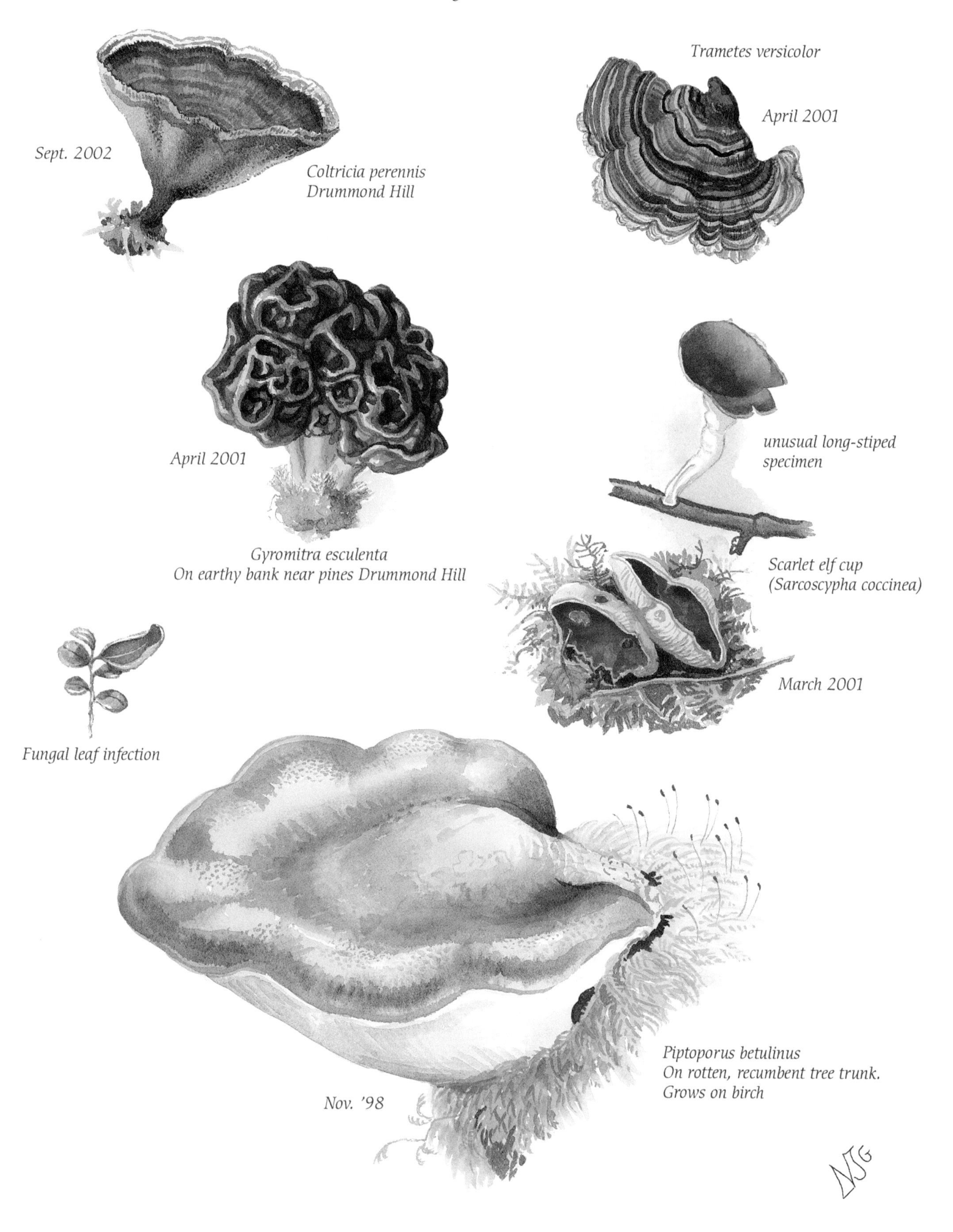

Trametes versicolor
April 2001
Sept. 2002
Coltricia perennis
Drummond Hill
April 2001
unusual long-stiped
specimen
Gyromitra esculenta
On earthy bank near pines Drummond Hill
Scarlet elf cup
(Sarcoscypha coccinea)
March 2001
Fungal leaf infection
Piptoporus betulinus
On rotten, recumbent tree trunk.
Grows on birch
Nov. '98

*Sketch of Bluebells near Garth Castle, June 2001*

April 2000
Flowering twig
Common ash
(Fraxinus excelsior)
1967

May 2000
Bird cherry
(Prunus padus)
Portbane potting shed
with Bird cherry
May 2000
Wild cherry, Gean
(Prunus avium)

Apple
May 2001
Crab apple
Portbane
garden
NJG

*Coal tits on Larch*

Mosses - April 2001

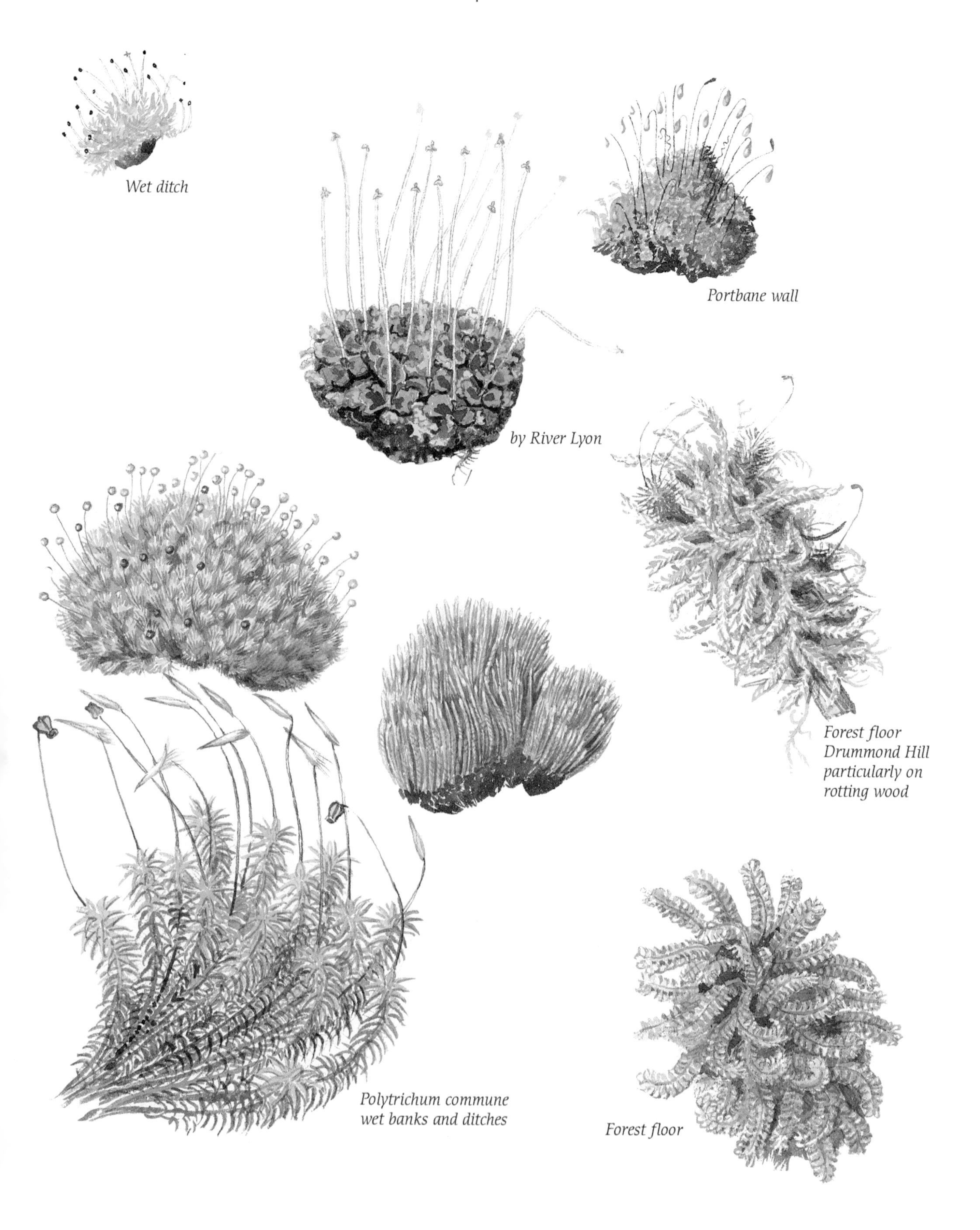

*Ancient Scots pine above Tombuie Cottage* Oct. '97

# Black Wood of Rannoch

Under the hill
By the black bog quaking
Great trees stand, tufted thick,
Rose infused, python-glossy
Along their limbs; rough bark flaking.
The ground between cushioned deep
With blaeberry, hillocked heath,
Aromatic juniper, moss
And mounded wood-ant heap.
A place still haunted
By cork-pop caper cocks;
Stag frequented and
Intensely still.

*Young cock capercaillie*

*Woolly rhinoceros*

# The Forest

The ice cap and glaciers of the Ice Age formed Drummond Hill just as they scooped out Loch Tay and the glens and corries in the surrounding mountains. The hill was a long narrow mica-schist barrow beneath, and later between, the grinding ice of two glaciers. There must have been mammoths and woolly rhinos in earlier interglacial periods in this part of Scotland, but they died out here before the glaciers retreated for the last time about 10,000 years ago. As the ice receded it was replaced by dwarf willow and tundra lichens, mosses and grasses. There were great migrations of reindeer, and herds of wild horses would have roamed below the hill over the alluvial flats of Strath Appin which were often flooded by melt-water as the glaciers shrank. On the shingley banks of the young rivers Tay and Lyon, vast flocks of cranes, geese, swans and ducks came to breed and filled the land with their tumultuous voices. In the water were leaping silver hordes of salmon and seatrout, so that often the air was heavy with the scent of living fish, as it can be even today during their Spring and Autumn runs from and to the sea.

*Prehistoric wild horse*

Gradually, as the climate warmed, the greater beasts of the ice age disappeared and forests replaced the tundra; forests of alder, birch, ash and oak, rowan and holly, wych elm, hazel, Scots pine, juniper and yew. In the forests lived brown

*Mammoths*

*European bison*

bears, wolves, lynx, elk ('moose' to Americans), red-deer and roe-deer, wild boar, bison, and the great aurochs (ancestor of our domestic cattle) whose trumpeting bellows echoed through the trees. Capercaillie and black grouse haunted the forest and its edges, while along the watercourses beavers fed upon the bark of aspen, alder and goat willow and at the same time they formed by their activities new alluvial pockets where these trees could flourish.

Hunters of the Old Stone Age, who moved north after the receding ice, gradually became Neolithic, then Bronze Age and Iron Age farmers – the Picts*, who thousands of years ago erected the stone circles still to be seen near Drummond Hill, the cup-marked boulders and cysts on the hillsides of which there are many, and the crannogs in Loch Tay which were in existence 5,000 years ago (and still sometimes used until the early 17th century). Perhaps it was not lost on those early inhabitants that Drummond Hill is situated almost exactly in the true centre of mainland Scotland, and with the fertility of the soil and richness of wild life it is perhaps not surprising that the area was chosen as a centre for Pictish life and worship.

*Prehistoric standing stones, Tirinie.*
*Tirinie means 'place of corn'*

*The Picts (or Pictii) may have been a name applied to a particular tribe of aboriginal inhabitants by the Romans. But here I use it to stand for all the earliest inhabitants of Scotland.

Although all this seems a long time ago there are many links between now and then in Nature; for much of its ancient glory still lives in Scotland like embers damped down but alive, and waiting to be re-kindled.

---

When the Romans came to this part of Scotland they are said to have built a fort on the eastern end of Drummond Hill (where there are the remains of a prehistoric dun, or hill-fort), and a camp at Fortingall, where there was already the settlement of a Pictish king, and where local tradition has it that Pontius Pilate was born. Some of the Fortingall remains have proved to be medieval, but a Roman staff was found there and the medieval township could have been superimposed upon earlier remains. The Romans exported bears from the forests of Scotland to Rome for their savage circus 'games'.

Not long after the Scots had invaded the Pictish lands from the west, and when Christianity was just beginning to spread in Scotland, the Romans left; unable to conquer such a wild land and people even after four hundred years in Britain. The forests then began increasingly to be felled, a process which had been begun thousands of years earlier. The bear and the aurochs disappeared. Wood from the forests was used for smelting iron and other metals, for building ships and for

*Prehistoric crannog*

European brown bear

gain, and the forest was also cleared for agriculture. The country slowly took on a more open aspect and the goats of an increasing human population slowed regeneration of trees. The raising of cattle became widespread, with the accompanying cattle-rieving between clans. Wolves, presumably owing to predation on this livestock, were heavily persecuted, the last one in the area being killed, tragically, on Rannoch Moor in the 18th century. It is said that the last beaver had already been killed for its skin in the 14th century, an illustration among many others that people do *not* necessarily 'conserve' what is of value to them, and for this reason the modern conservation catchword 'use it or lose it' is suspect.

Through the 17th and 18th centuries, great cattle-drovers' trysts were held below the open slopes of Drummond Hill where thousands of cattle were bought and sold – many of them to be walked to England as far away as London. The drovers had a special breed of tail-less dog of which old breed a representative still lived until recently in the neighbourhood, belonging to Mr and Mrs McLaughlan of Ardtalnaig. These tail-less dogs also exist on the Welsh borders, where they too are known to be descended from the drovers' breed.

European beaver

In those days small fields of flax, roots, hay, oats and barley chequered the lochside, straths and glens, ploughed by ponies, or dug and harvested by hand, so that there was much to be gleaned by wild birds and animals. Cattle were moved to the hills in summer where butter and cheeses were made, and flax spun, by the women and girls. Millers, weavers, lime-kilners, blacksmiths, shoemakers, boat-builders, wheelwrights, journeymen, tailors, drovers and tinkers plied their trades amidst a fairly extensive rural population. But the braes and burn-banks were still stippled with woods of sparkling birch, rowan and hazel, and there were many open forests of oak and alder, or of Scots pine and juniper with their spongey carpets of blaeberry, mosses and heather. The local people depended upon these woods to supply them with barrel-staves, hurdles, walls, doors, house supports,

Naturally tail-less breed
of drover's dog

Some cattle to the Tryst

roof timbers, bowls, tools, furniture, boats, pack-saddles, dies and firewood, nuts and mast, and forage for their animals. Access to the woods was valued.

Then came the enclosures and clearances. The small open fields began to disappear, stone walls were built, and the hills became speckled with a scurf of sheep. Birches, hollies, oaks, pines and rowans gradually stopped regenerating, and in places where heather was overgrazed by the sheep it began to retreat, although some grassy hills have characterised this area for a very long time, where the earth is calcerious rather than acidic.

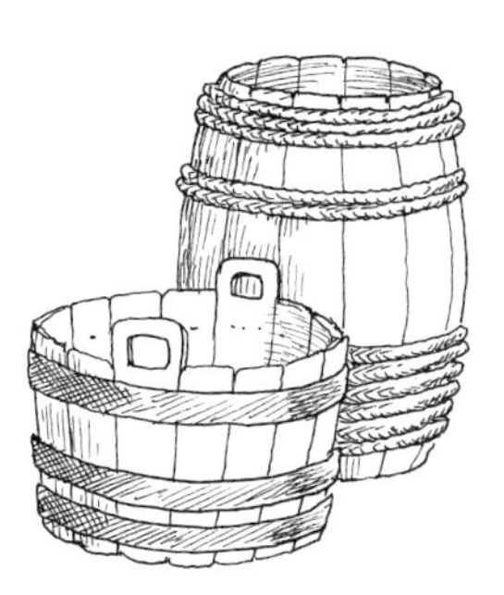

*Wooden tub and barrel*

The Victorian landlords' new penchant for large shoots of grouse and pheasants (which still lingers today) and the employment of gamekeepers to ensure a surplus of 'game' to feed the guns, caused an unprecedented and great decline in the diversity and number of other wild life that was not 'game', in the forests and on the hills. Another Victorian fashion inimical to wild life was egg-collecting and the stuffing of specimens. The Scottish capercaillie had already recently become extinct and the polecat became so. The pine marten and Scottish wildcat almost disappeared too. The red kite, gosshawk, eagle owl and greater spotted woodpecker died out as breeding birds in Scotland – the sea eagle and osprey soon thereafter. But as early as 1837–38 Lord Breadalbane of Taymouth Castle had already reafforested Drummond Hill and re-introduced the capercaillie there from Sweden. After 25 years these had increased to about 1000 birds. The greater spotted woodpecker began to return at the end of the 19th century and to recover slowly through the first half of the 20th.

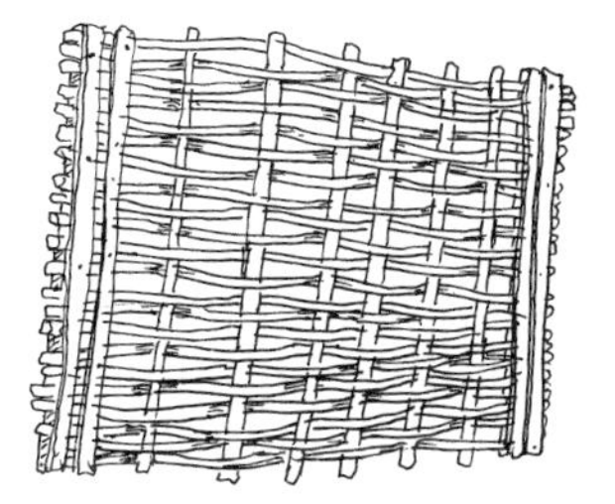

*Hurdle used for building*

With the World Wars came the final cutting of many of the remaining woods in the area including most of the trees on Drummond Hill and Gunpowder Hill, though a few patches of ancient pines survived. Since the last war, new commercial

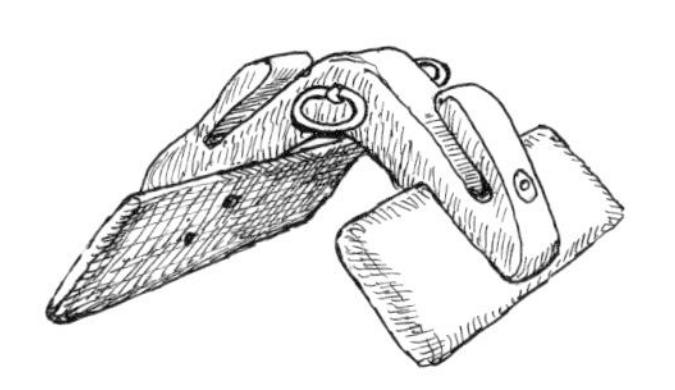

*Wooden pack saddle*

*Old Scots pine*

*Goshawk*

*A big Noble fir – American Garden, Taymouth*

forests of conifers have been planted and Drummond Hill is covered with trees once more. Recently, some of the remaining areas of natural woodland in the locality have been fenced to encourage regeneration and other areas have been replanted with native trees; including Gunpowder Hill, by its enlightened owner.

Below Drummond Hill at the eastern end of the loch between the road and the shore, is an arboretum of magnificent trees. They were planted well over a hundred years ago, perhaps in 1800, when the Castle gardens were moved near there, by the Campbell of Breadalbane of that time, and they have reached immense size – many having a girth of between twenty and thirty feet, the largest presently thirty-four feet in circumference measured well above the flare of the roots. There are noble firs, Douglas firs, sequoias, Wellingtonias, redwoods, cedars, an Araucanian pine, deodars and morinda spruces from the Himalaya, and others. This arboretum was a patch of wilderness where very little 'tidying' or interference had occurred for a long time. Lately, though, some of the woodland of native trees that had grown up around the old giants has been cleared and perhaps they will do all the better for this. The walled and long-disused vegetable and flower garden of Taymouth Castle, next to the 'American Garden' (or arboretum) where these trees grow, used also to be a wilderness, good for butterflies and wild flowers including chickory, mallow and Jacob's ladder. It was entered through a beautiful wrought iron gate in the ivy-covered wall. Now the garden space is crammed with tidy 'timeshare' houses, and the gate, the ivy and the wild flowers have gone. Wilma Carlin of Kenmore told me that when the ruined green-houses of this garden were demolished to make way for the timeshare cottages, large numbers of hedgehogs which had been living beneath them were displaced and many perished on the nearby road. But now house martins and swallows can build under the eaves of the new houses if allowed (indeed, it is illegal to clear away swallow's and martin's nests until the breeding season has finished. They cannot legally be cleared away even while they are being built and before eggs have been laid).

*Hedgehog*

Some huge larch trees which characterised Taymouth castle grounds and nearby hills in the past are still alive, though many have now been felled. The larch tree is said to have been introduced to the area from Europe in the 17th century by Black Duncan Campbell of Balloch (later Taymouth) and now there are Japanese larches and their hybrids on Drummond Hill as well. Although not truly 'native', larch provides important food for siskin, tit, crossbill, red squirrel and others. The beech tree too was not native but has been extensively planted and self seeded, perhaps brought originally from England. All trees do well in the yellow, glacial and often calcarious loam of this area and grow to be large, some local beeches having a girth of fifteen feet or more. In years when beeches bear a heavy

*Wood pigeons*

*Cone eaten by squirrel*

crop of mast (some years they have none) our own big wood pigeons and the flocks of smaller and darker immigrant wood pigeons from Scandinavia find plenty to eat. At these times, whenever you stop under a beech tree over fifty years old (they are said seldom to bear mast before this age) an explosion of pigeons occurs as they leave precipitately. Red squirrels and mice, jays and many other birds including capercaillies and pheasants benefit from beech nuts, and tits carry them off one by one to eat or to poke into crevices for future use. For anyone who takes the trouble to open the small, three-sided nuts and scrape away the furriness inside, they are delicious. It seems a strange waste of the tree's energy to produce flowers and nut cases even in a year when no mast ripens, but presumably the ripening depends on triggers which occur later in the year so that the trees cannot 'know' in advance.

*Wood beetle*

A beautiful tree in spring, with lime-green pom-poms of winged seeds that appear very early after the pink and mauve tufted flowers, and before the leaves are properly unfurled, is the wych elm – a tree native to Scotland which replaces here the common elm of England (which was in fact originally introduced from Europe, perhaps by the Romans). We hoped the wych elms would be immune to Dutch elm disease – a disease thought, in fact, to come from the Far East – for they did not show signs of it for a long time after it had already decimated the common elms in England. But now nearly all the big wych elms have died and you can see the patterns of the galleries of the elm bark beetle, associated with spreading the disease, on the bark-less trunks of the dead trees. Whych elm saplings, before they develop rough bark, are not affected however. Some elms in England, Holland and America are resistant to the disease, so perhaps in time the wych elm will develop resistance too. But for now it is a loss to red squirrels, which depended on the early seeds of wych elm to augment their spring diet (incidentally, I have seen them also enjoying the flowers of sycamore which are full of nectar). Dead and hollow trees killed by disease, if not cleared away in the interests of 'tidiness' or 'safety', provide insect food for woodpeckers and other birds, and nest sites for many.

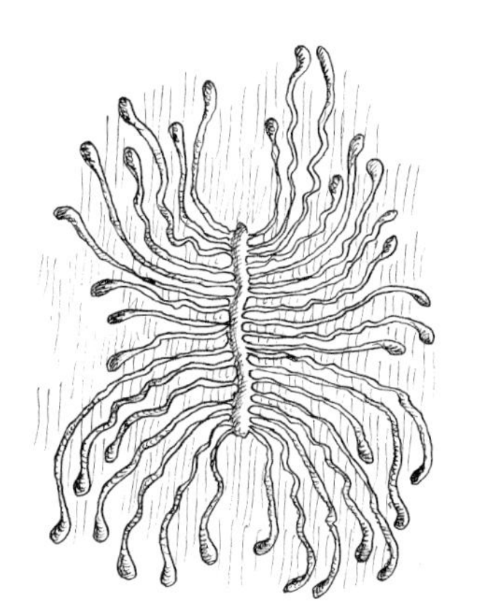

*Gallery pattern of elm bark beetle, associated with elm disease*

The sweet chestnut, possibly also first introduced to Britain by the Romans, must be beyond its natural range here, for although there are some big specimens they do not often develop fat nuts, and the prickly nut-cases lie empty and disappointing on the ground like tiny green hedgehogs. The horse chestnut too was not originally a native and thought to have come from Turkey.

*Sweet chestnut fruits*

Some other 'foreign' trees and shrubs naturalised on Drummond Hill and elsewhere in its vicinity are *Rhododendron ponticum*, Himalayan tree-cotoneaster, Himalayan honeysuckle, buddleia (very important for butterflies), red-berried elder, American elder and American rowan (which has crimson berries instead of scarlet). There is also Portuguese laurel and spurge laurel: and there are, of course, the commercially grown exotic conifers such as Norway spruce, sitka, western hemlock, balsam and Douglas firs, many of which put up seedlings and seem perfectly acclimatised to Scotland although some of these exotic firs are not very helpful to our native wild life, especially when closely planted. Siskins feed from the cones of thujas, and squirrels get seed from a number of different species. Crossbills also take an interest in spruce. Rhododendron, and Japanese knotweed (recently appeared), can both damage native plant diversity if allowed to ramp.

*Female capercaillie alert*

The yew, native and once common in Highland forests, is said to have almost died out owing to lack of regeneration with a return to colder conditions after the Romans left, although there are many ancient yews still alive such as the '3000 year old' tree at Fortingall, now considered to be much older – possibly even 9000 years old, and therefore perhaps the oldest living specimen of vegetation in Europe. The biggest yew tree I have ever seen is growing above Weem below the cliffs there; a magnificent, healthy giant that might be thousands of years old. Recently young juniper and yew saplings have appeared, seeded by birds. Their regeneration could be a positive aspect of global warming, which might also help the Caledonian Forest to return; for Scots pines, too, are said to prefer a slightly warmer, drier climate than we have had of late. However, it is still uncertain how this warming trend will effect the weather of Scotland for if the Gulf Stream shifts as a result of it, the last prediction of the Lady of Lawers, made in the 17th century, that the country around Ben Lawers will become too cold for anyone to live there, may yet be fulfilled: as have all her other prophecies. Recent research has indicated that some of the ice ages developed, or disappeared, in a matter of decades rather than over thousands of years as previously believed – so 'sudden' changes of climate have been characteristic of Scotland in recent geological time.

*Capercaillie chick*

When we began exploring Drummond Hill thirty-four years ago, few people walked there, and there were no mountains bikes then. The logs were cut with hand- saws and axes one at a time and wriggled out down narrow, steep paths by

*The very big yew tree at Weem, with my mother for comparison*

Clydesdale horses, which were brought to the forest in a cattle lorry. There was little disturbance or noise when tree-felling was in progress. Capercaillies were thriving and we often saw them; either rocketing explosively out of the tree-tops to fly off with a harsh whistle of wings or a silent glide, sitting in the branches, or walking on the ground with broods of sturdy chicks which could fly when they were still very small.

*Removing logs*

Capercaillies are said to sometimes 'damage' the leading shoots of young pines preventing the development of a long, straight tree, suitable for making planks. But many of the Scots pines in the old, native forests are of a spreading shape with branches nearly as thick as their trunks; this more typical shape perhaps stemming partly from early 'damage' by capercaillies and deer. Timber from these majestic trees is ideal for making things of beauty. Capercaillies, too, seem to prefer old, mature trees, and if these are available tend to leave young trees alone. But, presumably because of the perceived damage to the closely planted plantations, capercaillies soon began to be shot in the forest 'officially' and they were shot until recently in spite of very serious decline, and now the capercaillie has almost died out once more on Drummond Hill. There is little more thrilling than to see one of these great 'horses of the woods' and the Forestry Commission is now trying to improve conditions for them in the forests. For surely capercaillies on Drummond Hill (and elsewhere) are a greater national treasure than a few more straight planks? It will be sad if by the time this book is published capercaillies have disappeared altogether from Drummond Hill.

Something that I have not found on Drummond Hill is the wood ant although it is numerous in the Black Wood of Rannoch, with its household mounds of pine needles and sandy earth. Perhaps if these ants could be introduced to Drummond Hill they would improve the capercaillie's chance of survival: for the chicks, of course, are insectivorous – and adults are said to eat some insects in the winter. But I have not been able to discover if capercaillies do eat wood ants.

*Wood ant nest*

*Lonely capercaillie*

Capercaillies lived in other woods in the neighbourhood too, as they still do farther away. Mrs Joan Price of Bolfracks told me that during the First World War there was only one capercaillie left in the Bolfracks woods. This cock bird was so lonely that he came out of the forest to display to the domestic hens near the house.

On top of Drummond Hill near 'Revard' we used to come upon a circular stone construction hidden in thick undergrowth amongst the trees that we imagined to be the remains of a prehistoric dwelling. Lately it has been cleared and we learnt that, far from being prehistoric, it was the remains of an ice house used for storing ice through the summer for Taymouth Castle and used for that purpose to within the last sixty-five years. There used to be a pond near it, recently restored with a small dam, from which the ice was cut. This pond will be of use to the wild creatures of the hill, especially frogs and toads.

*Remains of the ice house*

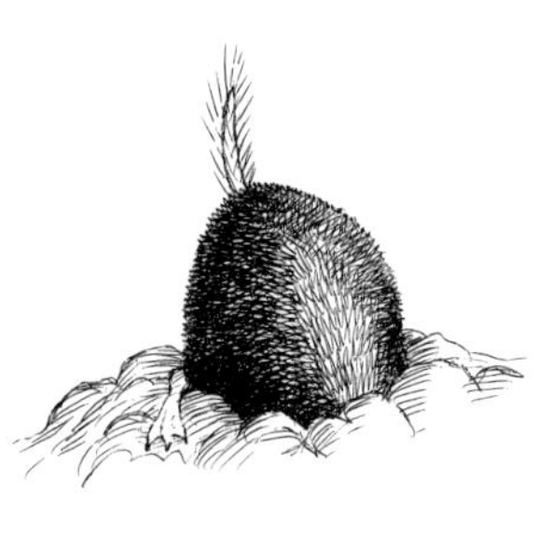

*Mole*

It is somehow surprising to find mole-hills on the top of Drummond Hill for its sides are so steep – though moles are much more active creatures than one might suppose, and the young ones are always emigrating in search of unoccupied territories where they will not be persecuted, or even killed, by their unsociable elders.

The breeding season of moles, as of so many other creatures, is in the spring when the pale, silky tuftlets are on the larches and the frilly new green of opening buds decorate the broad-leaved trees of Drummond Hill, and wood warblers chant their rich, melodious songs, accompanied by the merry 'ups and downs' of chiff-chaffs (a bird never very common here) and cascades of delicate notes from willow warbler, robin, song thrush and titmouse. While the foliage is yet light and new, tree trunks show through it, some rough and dark, others fluted, smooth or reticulated; rosey Scots pines and alders shining silver, and here and there the pure white of a birch. Amongst them in dusky contrast, shows the foliage of yew, spruce and fir. The whole forest, then, feels blythe and cool.

*Opening broom pod*

When it is hot, and at times in the summer it can be as hot as Africa, and the light is flat and the hills look hard and bright or are nearly lost in heat-haze, the forest is redolent with the intoxicating scent of pine resin, and the opening of pine cones and the popping of sharply twisting broom pods followed by the rattle of their scattered seeds, like tiny grape-shot, can be heard everywhere. There is the rustle of common lizards along sun-catching banks on open stretches of forest track; and maybe a glossy slow-worm will be lying coiled in a pool of sun-light. Large dragon flies can be seen hawking over open spaces and the sleepy ticking of grasshoppers is still to be heard (now no longer the ubiquitous sound of summer it used to be). When bracken is tall and green, flies may swarm in the forest and a hat of bracken fronds helps to keep them off your face. Clegs steal like stealth bombers to stab with the blunt needles of their proboscidae and can chase one out of a patch of forest quickly: more frightening to me than wasp or adder. Along the edges of some of the paths, the now rare pearl-bordered fritillary flies low over blue-flowered bugle and pretty speckled-yellow moths flutter in the daytime, more like butterflies than moths. Sometimes thousands of rusty-coloured baby frogs and toads move up into the forest in summer.

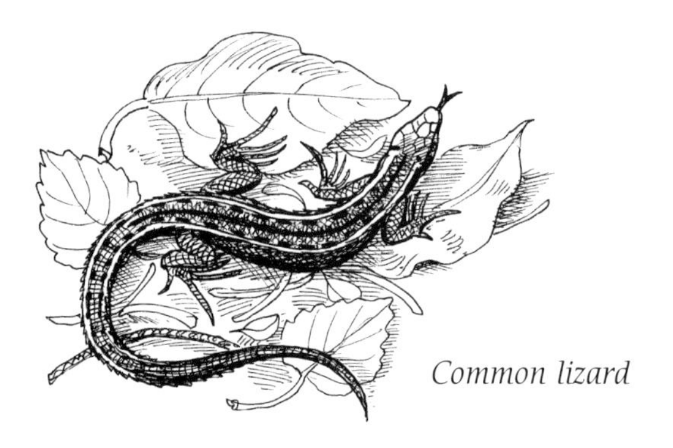

*Common lizard*

On the woodland tracks can be seen sometimes the droppings of fox, wildcat, pine marten, hedgehog, deer, and of the few sheep still living wild on the Hill; and rarely now, the cylindrical, spruce-needle-filled droppings of capercaillie. The large slugs that live in the forest eat many of these droppings, which must account in part for the relative scarcity of droppings to be found.

*Large horned roe buck*

After their breeding season small birds in the forest often gather in feeding-flocks and move steadily through the trees together, so that what at one moment was a silent, empty place is suddenly filled with movement and the calls of long-tailed, coal and great tits, chaffinch, siskin and tree-creeper, willow warbler and tiny goldcrest. They search tree trunks, twigs and leaves, cones and seed-capsules diligently for small insects, spiders or seeds. Books often mention the two white wing bars of the goldcrest, which are indistinct, but they fail to describe the dark, eye catching patch between these bars like the round, black spot on the flanks of certain yellow butterfly fish of coral reefs; and they do remind me of tiny tropical fish as they poke about the tree-reefs of their forest home.

Roe deer seem, with the capercaillie and red squirrel, to be the spirit of the woods made flesh. In winter their rough coats are grey and their tail patches pure white. But light can change this coat colour to an appearance of dark chocolate at times. In the summer, roe are glossy cinnamon red with ochre-yellow 'beacons'. These patches of white or yellow fur beneath the non-existent tail normally appear quite small but as soon as a deer is alarmed the hair spreads to become a large inverted heart-shape, very conspicuous as the animal bounds away up a hillside between the trees or down a forest ride, or moves through an umber autumnal dusk. Then, the pale patches are often all that can be seen of the deer, bobbing disembodied like fairy lanterns.

*Roe buck*

In mid-summer when roe are rutting, one can find on Drummond Hill and elsewhere, the perfect rings where bucks have chased coquetting does round and around with perhaps a small bush or rock as hub to their wheel.

*Roe's courting ring*

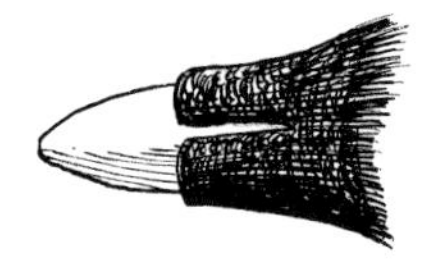

*Top-side of cock capercaillie's beak*

Deer enjoy eating holly, a tree which had become scarce but which is regenerating where sheep have been fenced out and deer reduced. Strangely, not every holly tree is browsed and I know of two growing side by side on Drummond Hill, one of which has been so much nibbled that it is like topiary. The other is untouched, of an open, slender shape, and has grown much taller, though I think both trees are the same age. Why is one palatable, the other not?

Mr Stott of Kenmore once found three roe deer curled up near each other, apparently asleep, amongst broom bushes on Drummond Hill. But they were all dead, with not a mark upon them. He wondered if broom under certain conditions might become deadly to deer, though normally they seem to browse broom with impunity. This applies to yew and ragwort which are deadly when dry but may be browsed when green by *some* animals, without ill effect.

---

There is a part of the forest that I call Capercaillie Wood where people seldom go and the pines are old, gnarled and spreading, from the time before plantations. The ground there is deep with soft hummocks of moss and blaeberry, and there are no sounds except for those made by birds and the wind soughing intermittently through pine needles. Between the trees are piles of red deer droppings for deer appreciate this place too, although they have been mostly shot-out on Drummond Hill. Sometimes you can find there a feather from the tail of a cock capercaillie. And there is peace – not the passive peace of a mere absence of sound and activity but a living, dynamic peace that seems to make one more truly alive and aware than it is possible to be anywhere else but in such wild places.

---

It is said that since before the Romans and through historical time in Scotland 99 per cent of woodlands have been destroyed. But when Highland forests regrow, as I believe they will to a large extent (and we have a wonderful example of what some of these were like in the Black Wood of Rannoch), the red deer will surely return to their true home therein – and perhaps, who knows, the wolf!

*Wolves*

*Sequoia or Coast Redwood (Sequoia sempivirens)*
*The American Garden or Arboretum, Taymouth, Kenmore*

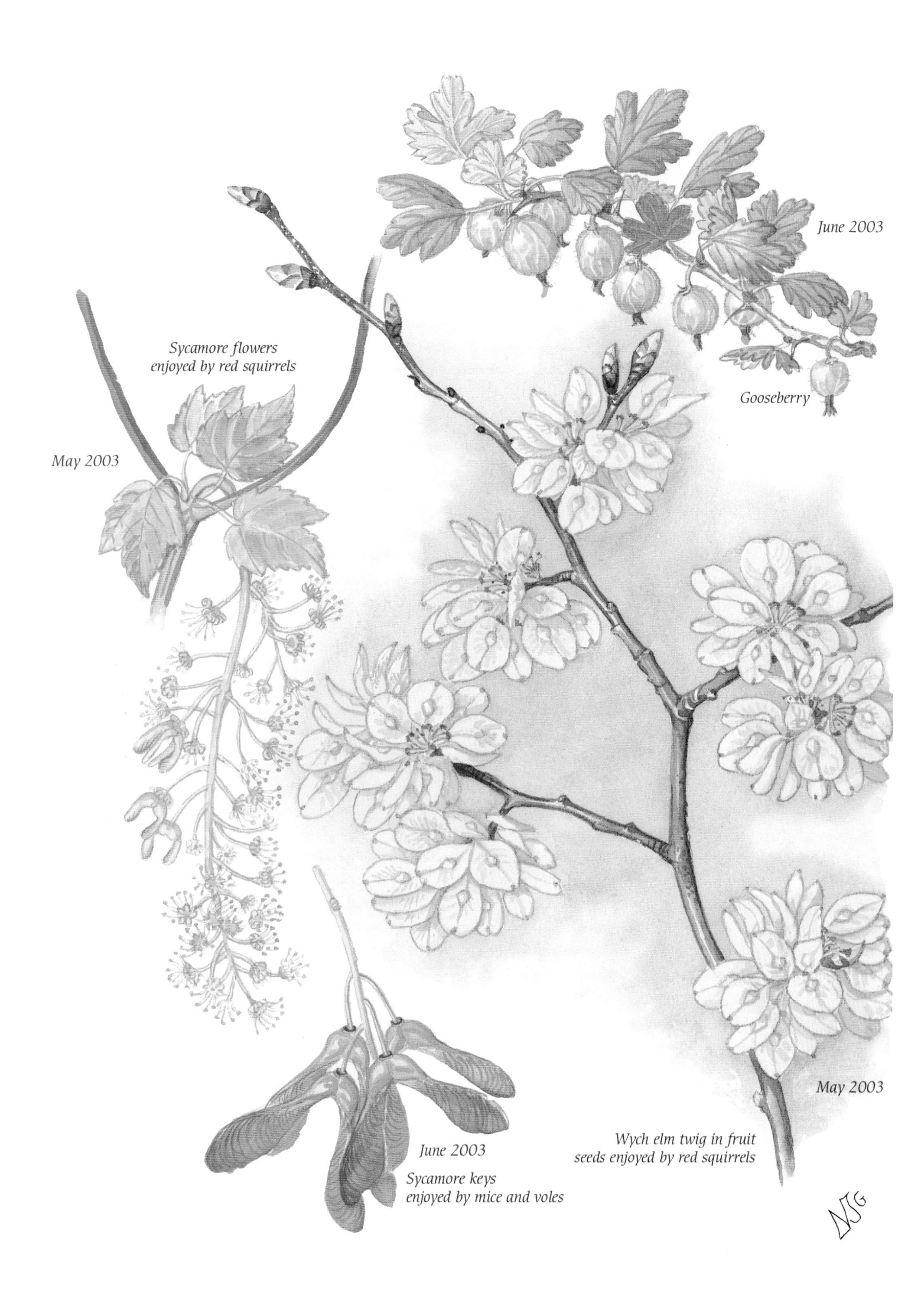
June 2003
Gooseberry
Sycamore flowers
enjoyed by red squirrels
May 2003
May 2003
June 2003
Sycamore keys
enjoyed by mice and voles
Wych elm twig in fruit
seeds enjoyed by red squirrels
NJG

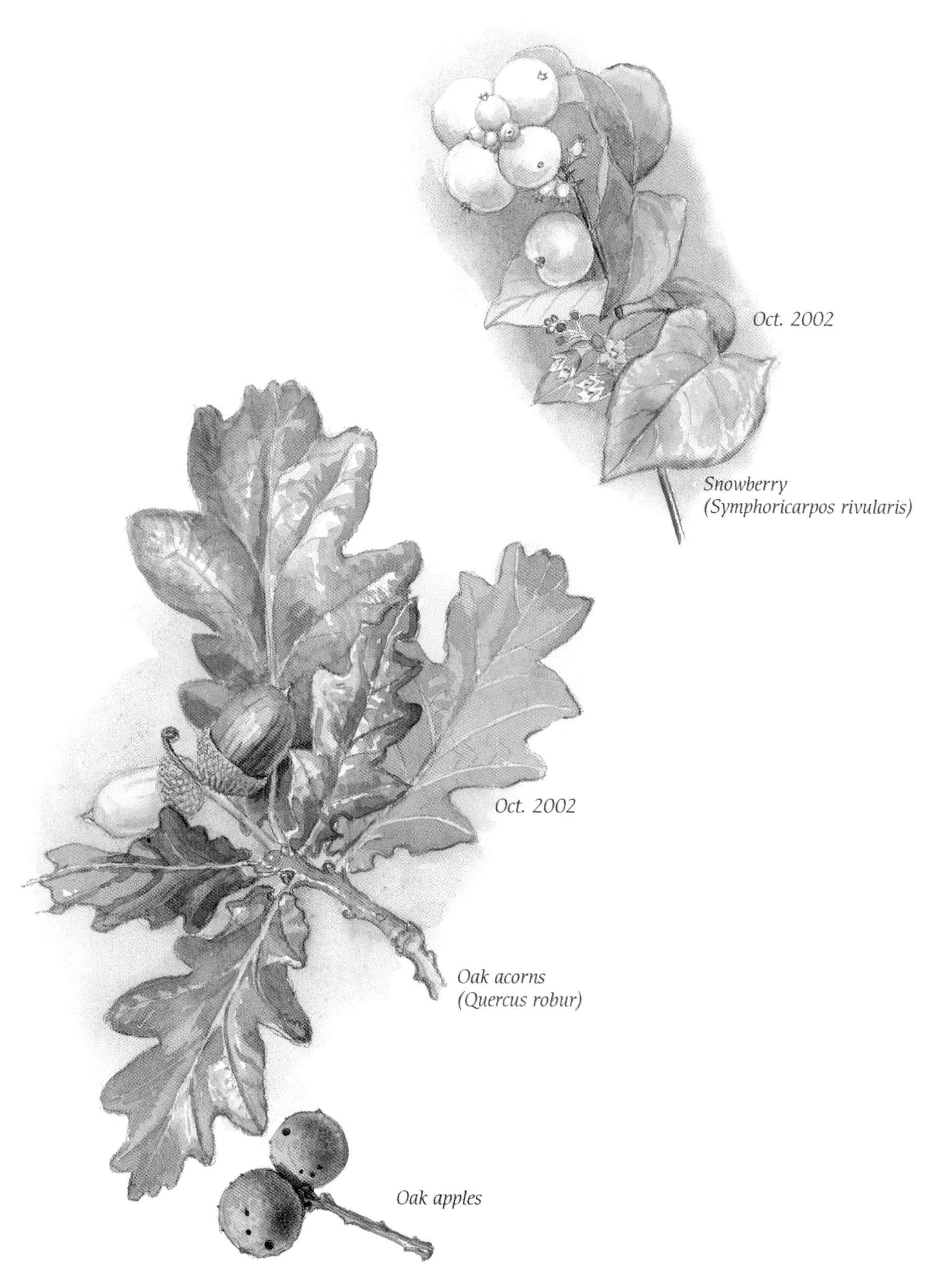
Oct. 2002
Snowberry
(Symphoricarpos rivularis)
Oct. 2002
Oak acorns
(Quercus robur)
Oak apples
NJG

*An old Buzzard's nest. Drummond Hill, Oct. '98*
*This tree broke in 1999*

*Portbane garden*

Scots pine
(Pinus silvestris)
Douglas fir
(Pseudotsuga menziesii)
Japanese larch
(Larix kaempferi)
Spruce
(Picea abies)
NJG

Scottish wild cats
4.5 x 4.5 cm
4.5 x 5 cm
Wild cat tracks in drainage ditch, Drummond Hill, Aug. '98
From life - sketches of wild cats
NJG

*Droppings (Mammals)*

*Roe deer*
*by Loch Tay*

*Nov. '97*

*Young Roe*
*Drummond Hill*

*Wild cat*
*Drummond Hill*

*Fox*
*Gunpowder Hill*

*March 2004*

*Red deer*
*Gunpowder Hill*

*Jan. '89*

*Stoat*
*Above Hazel Wood*

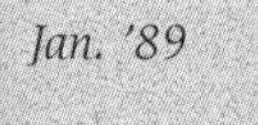

*Jan. '89*

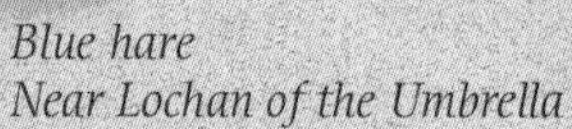

*Blue hare*
*Near Lochan of the Umbrella*

*Sept. '91*

*Pine marten, containing some hair,*
*a grain of wheat and semi-digested rowan berries*
*Drummond Hill*

*Young rabbit*
*The Hazels*

*Schiehallion from Drummond Hill,*
*Sept. '97*

*Some insects of Drummond Hill and surroundings*

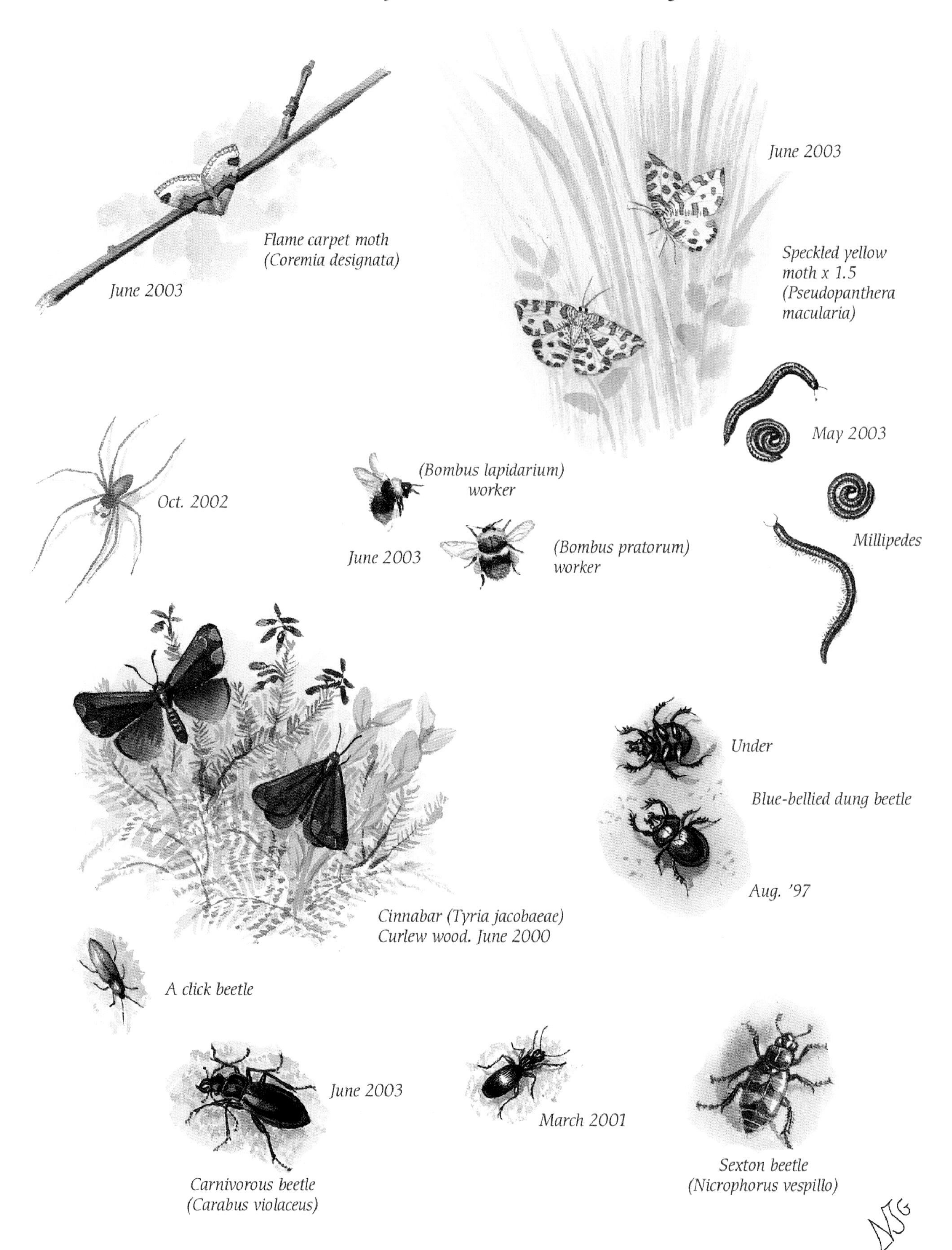

Sorbus aucuparia
(Rosaceae)
Rowan, Mountain Ash
Below: Sorbus americana
A rowan with crimson berries (instead of scarlet).
Naturalised on Drummond Hill
Sept. '97
garlic snail

Scots pine
(Pinus silvestris)
female flower
June 2000
male flower
male flowers
April 2001
Yew
(Taxus baccata)
male and female
flowers
June 2000
young cones
May 2000
Larch
(Larix decidua)
NJG

*Goldcrests on Larch, Nov. '98*

1, 3 and 5 Capercaillie (cock)
2 young Cuckoo
4 Buzzard
6 Hen Capercaillie (breast)
1
2
3
4
5
6
Oct. '97

*Cock Capercaillie, Drummond Hill, June 1980*

*Capercaillie droppings, Drummond Hill, Sept. '97*

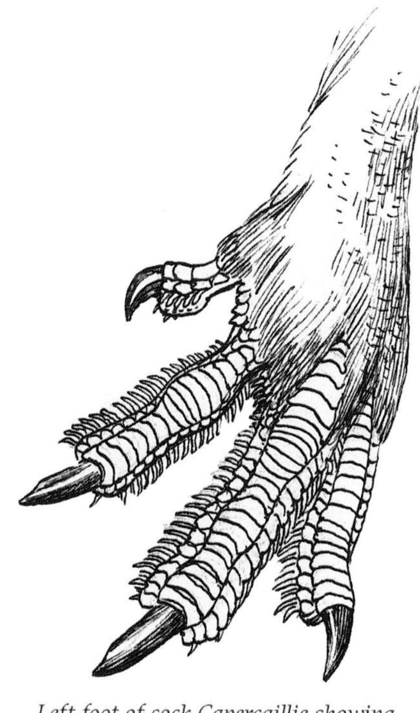

*Left foot of cock Capercaillie showing winter 'combs' on toes*

Peacock (Nymphalis oi)
Red Admiral (Vanessa atalanta)
Small tortoiseshell (Algais urticae)
Butterflies on
Buddleia (Buddleia davidii)
on Drummond Hill
Sept. 2002

## Butterflies

In the forest there was nothing much
Except tall firs on either side,
But sunshine filled the rides
And limned the grasses with a golden touch.
No creature moved, though small birds cried;
And I felt low to think, perhaps,
That all the animals had died.

But coming to an open hill
A single bush of buddlea, hung
With sprays of fragrant flowers,
Grew upon a tufted bank,
And to each spray butterflies clung,
More than I had seen for years:
Red admirals, Peacocks, Tortoiseshells.

The scented air was full of wings
Of movement and of fluttering
While I stood spellbound.
And all the time this thing I'd found
Filled me with such happiness
I walked on like a cat that sipped the cream,
Rapt in a contented dream.

*Red Admiral*

*Broom*

# Summer

When roadside elders are smothered with cream platters of musky-scented flowers, good to eat dipped in batter, fried, and sprinkled with sugar; and wild roses are coming out over banks where sweet cicely is in seed and bracken fronds have opened a green canopy; summer has arrived. It comes in slowly throughout June, most of which month remains spring-like. Because Drummond Hill is at the same high latitude as Kamchatka, the Aleutian Islands, Hudson's Bay and Northern Labrador, although because of the influence of the Gulf Stream on the climate this is not obvious, summer is short here.

Early morning mist on the loch means a hot day to come. Then the sun coaxes the broom flowers to diffuse a rich scent of peaches and the young sparkling leaves of the birches breathe out a fragrance of such sylvan beauty that it stops you in your tracks. Lasses used to wash their hair in a decoction of birch leaves in spring and early summer for the scent, and for the gloss it gave their tresses. Young birch leaves also make a clear yellow dye.

As summer advances it seems that there is less wild life to be seen for many of the birds are nesting and secretive, perhaps feeding second broods, and some have gone off to the forests to rear their young where they are more difficult to see

*Roe deer in the forest*

*Scots lass*

*Red squirrel scratching*

*Red deer calf*

amid the thickening foliage of the trees. Squirrels are harder to see too, and there is cover for roe deer. Red deer will be mostly away on the tops to give birth to their speckled calves where yellow bog asphodel will soon flower in the peat hags; although we have seen fat, glossy, summer hinds in the low woods of Glen Lyon and occasionally we used to see new, spotted calves with their mothers in the fields near Portbane.

Up in the hills male hen harriers display to their females on the nest in almost vertical rises and dives that leave one's tummy behind just to watch. They may do a series of these 'ups' and 'downs', reminiscent of the motion of a giant yo-yo. I hope, now that it is illegal to kill or interfere with these birds that this wonderful sight will be more often enjoyed.

---

In August 1968 I saw a heron over the Duneaves Road behind Drummond Hill tumbling about in the sky beset by rooks and crows. It was calling hoarsely and tossing a fish in its beak which it was trying to swallow. Later it achieved this and

*Hen harrier with loose feather*

*Heron mobbed by rooks and a crow for its fish*

the crows then flew away. But the heron continued for more than five minutes to fly aimlessly in large circles as if the incident had put out of its mind what it had meant to do next. The Duneaves road follows the River Lyon upstream from the bridge at the ruin of Comrie Castle and its verges are full of wild flowers in summer, with patches of yellow flags in boggy field corners. Along other roadsides too, that have not been prematurely and often unnecessarily cut by the ruthless machines of over-tidy councils, wood and meadow cranesbill open their lovely mauve and blue flowers, with water avens and herb bennet, while varnished buttercups, meadow sweet, lady's smock and oxeye daisies grow in the field edges. Some more unusual flowers of summer are fragrant orchid, butterfly orchid, bird's nest orchid, horse mint, live-long or orpine, alkanet, roseroot of the mountains and purple toadflax.

Even a summer ditch can be beautiful with wild flowers. Halfway up the track to the old Portbane Farm behind our house, water pulses from a drainage pipe laid under a steep field. It then flows along a ditch beside the track to the bottom of the hill where it passes under the road, through Portbane garden and into the loch. The water runs chuckling and bubbling, clear as Waterford glass, through beds of blue-flowered brooklime and forget-me-not and yellow flowered spearwort, its flow relatively constant, and damp even in the driest of summers. I saw small, round front-doors in the ditch-bank at water level, hidden amongst chickweed, and hoped that the now rare water vole was living there for it had recently been found along hill burns on Ben Lawers and elsewhere near Drummond Hill. But it is much more likely that these holes belonged to glossy

*Bringing down bracken*

chestnut bank voles which are quite numerous here. On my last visit the ditch had been cleaned out by a mechanical digger and had become a barren drain – but it will soon recover, as nature is strongly recuperative.

Each week of summer the bracken in The Hazels grows taller until it is hard work to push through chest-high fronds. Bracken used to be put to good use and was brought down on sleds and carts in the autumn as winter bedding for cattle in the byres. Other uses can be found for it today, whereby farmers could augment their income and keep bracken within bounds at the same time. Compost, to be sold to gardeners as an alternative to peat is one use to which it can be put. (The dried leafy stems are also good for keeping frost from more tender garden plants and shrubs over winter).

*Bracken*

*Cattle in the shade*

In August the foliage of trees is at its heaviest, with an almost blackish tinge to the green. Sheep and cows drowse in inky pools of fly-buzzing shade beneath the biggest oaks, sycamores and lime trees in the lower fields. Along field drains at the edges of the hills and beside the burns, red rattle, butterwort, lousewort, cow-wheat and spearwort are in flower. In sheep-nibbled turf there is wild thyme, alpine bistort, common speedwell, tormentil, heath bedstraw, eyebright and many other small flowers; while on slopes of wiry hill grasses, scabious, harebell, and yarrow are attracting butterflies: common blues, green-washed fritillaries and small and large heaths. The first green hairstreak butterfly I ever saw was on May 2nd 1988. On the way down Gunpowder Hill I saw something small and moth-like flutter to a stone. When near enough I saw it was a butterfly with a wingspan of less than an inch, and brilliant emerald-green underwings crossed by a chain of tiny white dots. It lay with its wings folded over its back almost quite on its side to absorb the sunshine. Green hairstreaks deposit their eggs on rock-rose, and there have always been egg-yolk-yellow rock-roses on that part of the hill – the caterpillars also eat blaeberry leaves.

*Bog myrtle*

Ringlet butterflies, a few meadow browns, pearl-bordered and greenwashed fritillaries are found in the fields, on hillsides and in boggy places amongst ragged robin and grass of Parnassus; and speckled woods – newly arrived, having increased their range recently – pearl bordered fritillaries, and green-veined whites fly along the forest rides of Drummond Hill. In moments of sunshine between cloud, velvet-winged Scotch arguses dance at grass height amongst bog myrtle at the edges of woods on the hillsides, whilst small coppers are to be found in gardens. Red admirals have a habit of floating high above ash trees or chasing each other with a fierce rattle of wings at flowering buddleias, while small tortoiseshells sun themselves in sheltered spots by the stone walls. An occasional painted lady, migrant from the south, flies fast and low over open places. In early summer there are often good numbers of orangetips in the area. Perhaps butterflies are increasing here after the depressing decline of the nineteen sixties, seventies and eighties, and amidst continuing worry about their future, for they remain vulnerable to bad weather and destruction of their food plants by farmers, gardeners and councils, and to agricultural chemicals. Recently I counted fifty-six peacock and red admiral butterflies on two flowering buddleia bushes on Drummond Hill one September afternoon. Among the prettiest of wild things, butterflies are an indication that all is well with nature. When they grow scarce something is wrong.

Moths, too, are on the wing in the honeysuckle-scented evenings of summer, evading the pipistrelles which flitter fast against a sky which is never wholly dark. Very long evenings that merge almost imperceptibly with the slow and very early return of light before dawn, is another of the lovely things about summer in the Highlands. During the shortest nights it is almost possible to read at any time by the light of the sky alone. It seems a pity to have to go in, and to bed, at all.

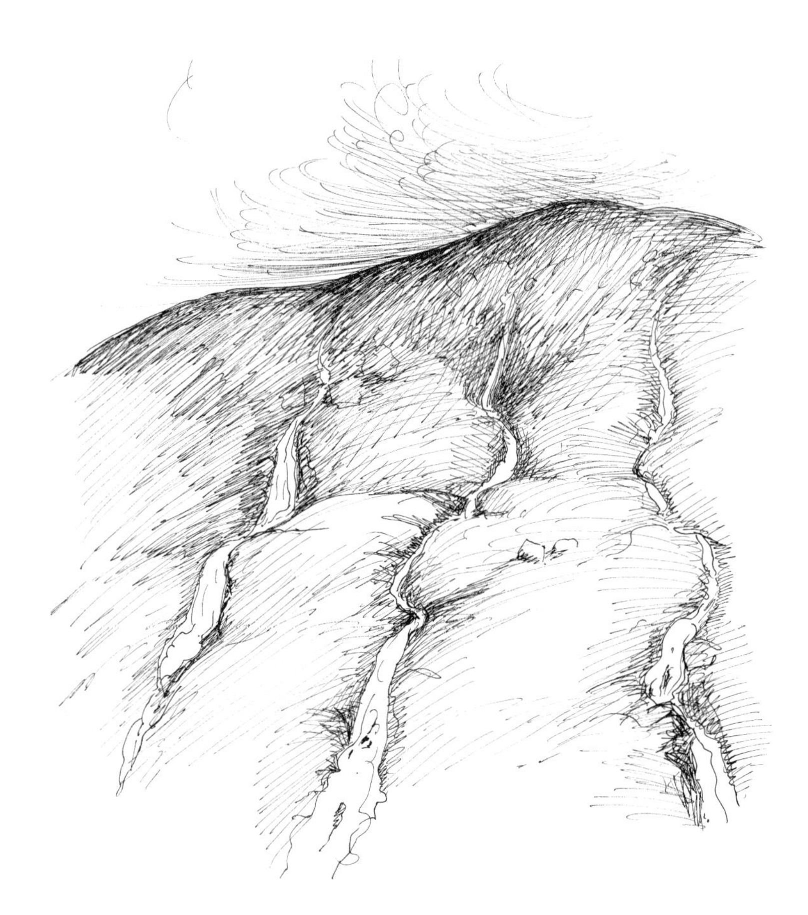

*Burns in spate like hanks of white wool*

*Rock pool*

On damp summer days delicious scents of flowers and leaves permeate the air that on dry days one would not notice. Rain often patters on the leaves or pelts in thundery deluges in the summer, when the burns fill and come down in cream-coloured torrents looking from a distance like hanks of new-spun wool draped on the mountains; or where the white spray leaps above the burns, like flocks of wild, exultant sheep galloping down the hillsides. From Portbane we sometimes hear the Remony and Acharn burns roaring like trains when they are in spate. But even in spates there must be safe holts in the burn-beds for the small, dark, burn trout to lie in, their flanks fizzed by bubbles and moved now and again by exhilarating tugs of current.

Occasionally summer can be bleak on the hills when the vertical columns of rain, sometimes peppered with hail, scurry over the treeless steeps like driven wraiths, and pipits and wheatears shelter behind tussocks, and water-drops slide down the whiskers of disconsolate blue hares crouched among the rocks.

In August some of the hills are suddenly covered in flowering heather; heather as spectacular and lovely as the earlier bluebells were, peopled with golden burrowing-bees and honey bees put out to 'graze'. Scottish heather honey is perhaps the best

*Bumble bee queen*

*Bee hive*

honey in the world but honey bees are not native to Scotland, because the bee queens do not normally survive winter in the wild, unlike the native bumble bee queens. So whenever honey bees are seen, a beekeeper with his hives is not far off. But occasionally a swarm will move into a roof or attic and survive as a colony there. Our great aunt Eva Blair, who lived within sight of Stirling's Wallace monument, had a huge colony of bees in the attic of her house which accumulated a great quantity of honey and comb over many years. I remember being chased by some of these bees when I was a little girl. They could certainly have been classed as wild for no-one looked after them or interfered with them until the old house was demolished years later.

*Honey bees*

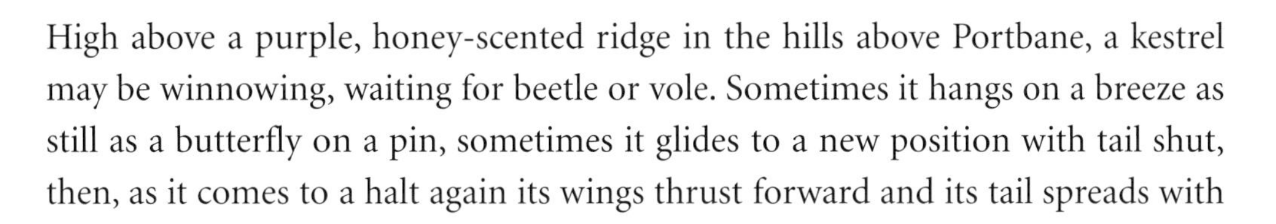

High above a purple, honey-scented ridge in the hills above Portbane, a kestrel may be winnowing, waiting for beetle or vole. Sometimes it hangs on a breeze as still as a butterfly on a pin, sometimes it glides to a new position with tail shut, then, as it comes to a halt again its wings thrust forward and its tail spreads with

*Kestrel hovering*

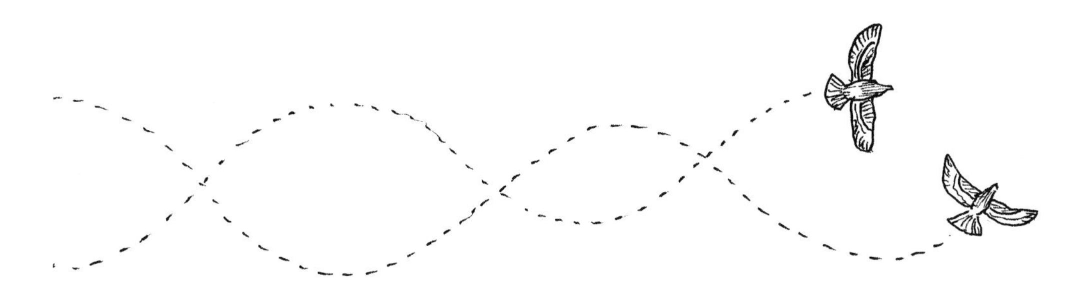

*Buzzards 'scissor-gliding'*

lovely deliberateness. Buzzards, playing with their newly fledged and flying young, mew and circle. Perhaps the lithe form of a merlin flicks fast and low over the heather, or a metallic 'chipping' song from a rocky burn heralds a fleeting ring ouzel or 'mountain blackbird', although they seem to have almost disappeared nowadays. Once I saw a pair of fieldfares in August and wondered if they were breeding here – a rare thing.

*Ring ousel*

Great flocks of rooks go up in late summer to feed on ripe blaeberries on the flanks of Gunpowder Hill, leaving the fruits that are sheltered beneath canopies of spider's web, however. Their droppings are stained mauve at this time but I have not found mauve red-grouse droppings and assume, perhaps wrongly, that for some reason they do not eat blaeberries. Perhaps this is because blaeberry is a woodland plant that grows on the hill where woods used to be – and the red-grouse being a bird of open moorland, perhaps had no opportunity until 'recently' to eat them. It is such conservative creatures, unlike the catholic rooks, that have difficulty adapting to change.

*Red grouse*

*Curlew*

In August hazel bushes are already covered with cream-coloured nuts, each with a rosy side nearest the sun.

*Cluster of hazel nuts*

Many of the mechanical conveniences we have lately acquired in civilised life seem to me not worth the sacrifice of quiet. Cars continually hurry by in summer, even lorries, although the road along the southern side of Loch Tay is too narrow for them. Strimmers, chain saws, mechanical hedge-clippers, mowing machines, radio, television, telephones, amplified music-machines, motor boats and jetskis on the loch make noise all summer long. Airforce jets scream down the glens while other 'planes pass higher overhead. Sometimes, even by Drummond Hill, it is impossible to hear birds singing. By contrast, while walking down the road near Portbane one summer evening when no machine could be heard, there was the faintest sound in the grass by the roadside. Looking down I found it had been a dandelion falling, cut by a chestnut bank vole who was now busily eating its stem. A black-cap was singing his last songs of the afternoon, a little squeakily to begin with but rounding out towards the end of each phrase into rich, mellow notes of

*Blackcap singing*

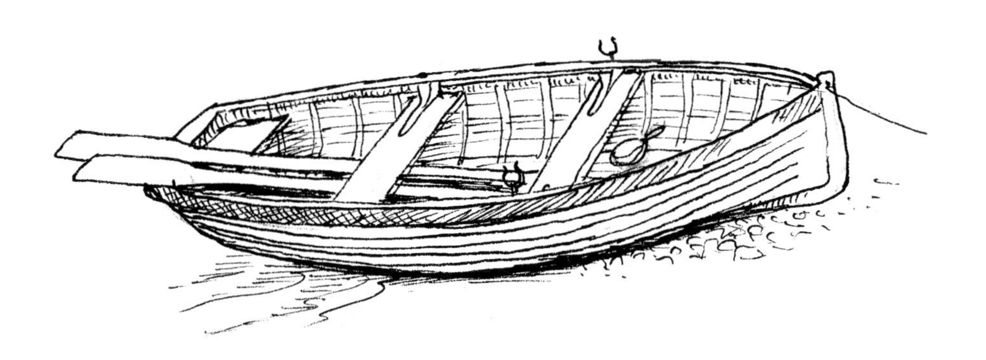

*Loch Tay fishing boat*

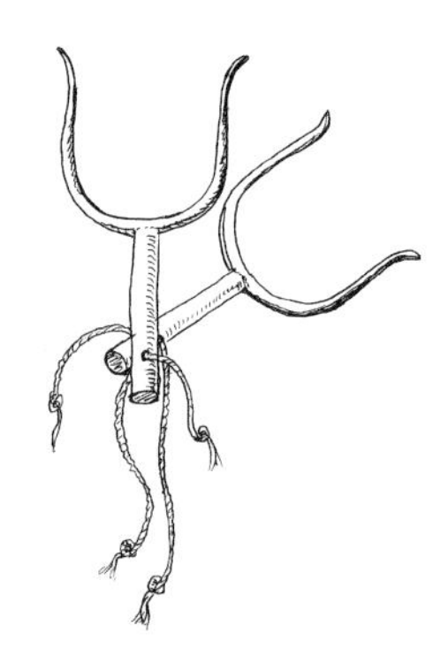

*Rowlocks*

great beauty. From the hill came the liquid call of a curlew, and from the loch the muted rhythm of oars in rowlocks as someone rowed unhurriedly on the calm water. When there is quiet of this nature the world seems to spread out wider and wider, and into the great spaces of it seeps Peace.

Another blessing mentioned earlier, but often, I think, not properly appreciated, is darkness and the slow changes of light to dark and of dark to light. But so often electric lights blaze unnecessarily all night, even outside in the summer in the country. Yet what could be more restful than darkness or more gentle than the gloamings of summer dawn and dusk in Scotland? Yet how many people hardly experience them for living by the blessing and the curse of electric light?

Standing outside the house one evening in summer, the sky pink, the loch a pale milky blue reflecting a yellow moon, I heard a click on the lochside stones. A roe was picking her way delicately along the water's edge, unaware she was watched. Already pipistrelles were out, flittering fast in the dusky gaps between

*Pipistrelles at dusk*

alder trees and over my head. The murmur of mallards came from farther out on the water, an occasional chatter of oystercatchers, and from the darkening bulk of Drummond Hill the first owl calls drifted. As the pink faded from the sky it was replaced by translucent green, and prickling stars began to appear. As it became darker Drummond Hill stood, long and black, its crest serrated with pines, like the back of a huge dinosaur. Against its reflection the rises of trout showed silver, coming and going rhythmically as the fish took water-flies from the surface. Gradually the moon, as it rose higher, shrank and became silver too, and I could see night-flying insects, beetles and moths, above the silhouettes of the lochside trees.

*Rises coming and going*

*Skylark singing*

*Hawthorn (Crataegus monogyna), May*

*Flowering Hawthorns in The Hazels, June*

*Hawthorn berries, 'haws'. Sept. '97*

*June 2000*

Rowan, mountain ash
(Sorbus aucuparia)
Guelder rose (Viburnum opulus)
June 2000
June 2003
(Species?)

American elder
(Sambucus canadensis)
May 2000
Elder
(Sambucus nigra)

*Some wild flowers of June*

Some wild flowers of July
July 2000
Tufted vetch
(Vicia cracca)
Yellow flag
(Iris pseudacorus)
Meadow crane's-bill
(Geranium pratense)
Fox-and-cubs
(Hieracium aurantiacum)
NJG

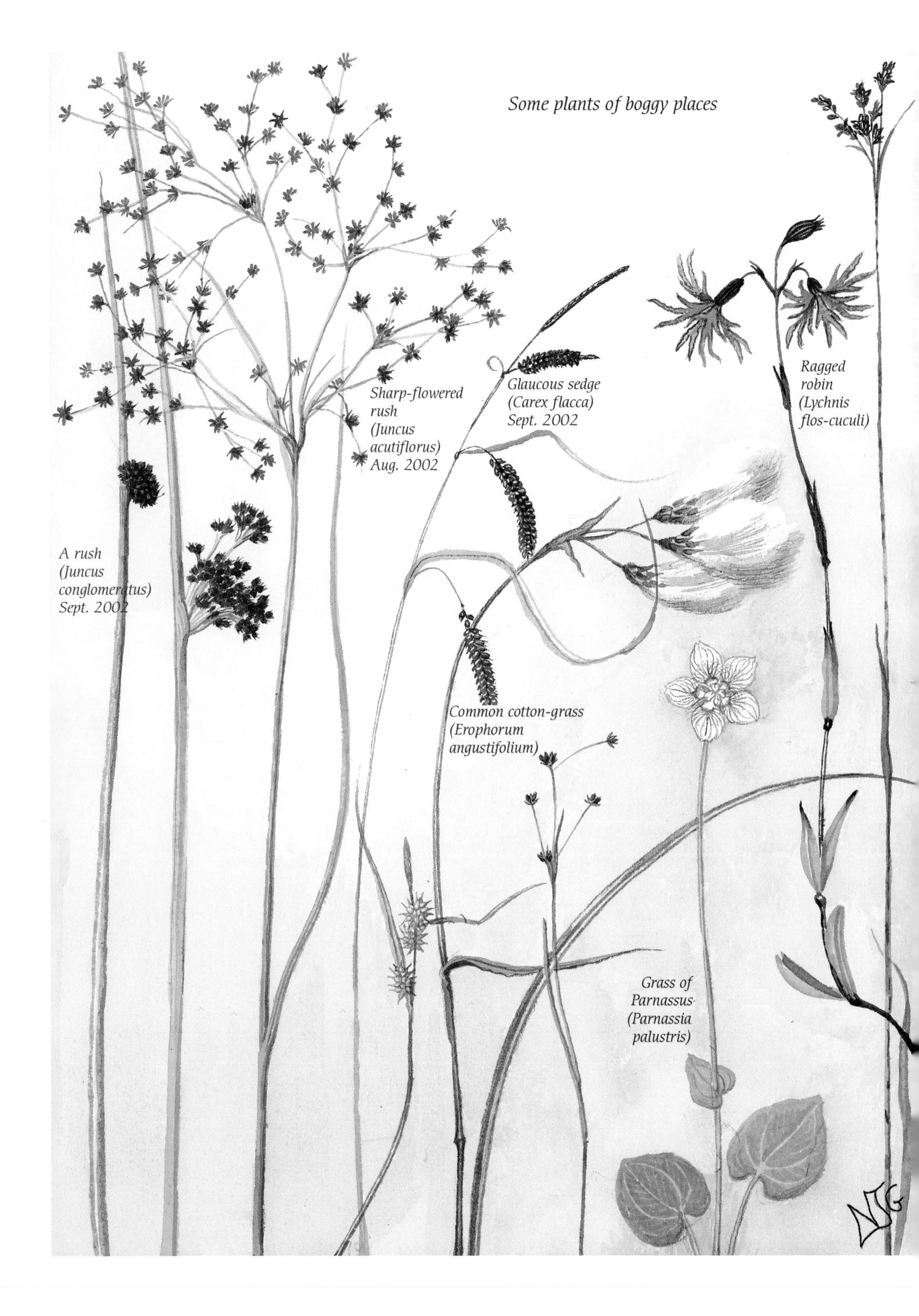
Some plants of boggy places
Sharp-flowered rush (Juncus acutiflorus) Aug. 2002
Glaucous sedge (Carex flacca) Sept. 2002
Ragged robin (Lychnis flos-cuculi)
A rush (Juncus conglomeratus) Sept. 2002
Common cotton-grass (Erophorum angustifolium)
Grass of Parnassus (Parnassia palustris)
NJG

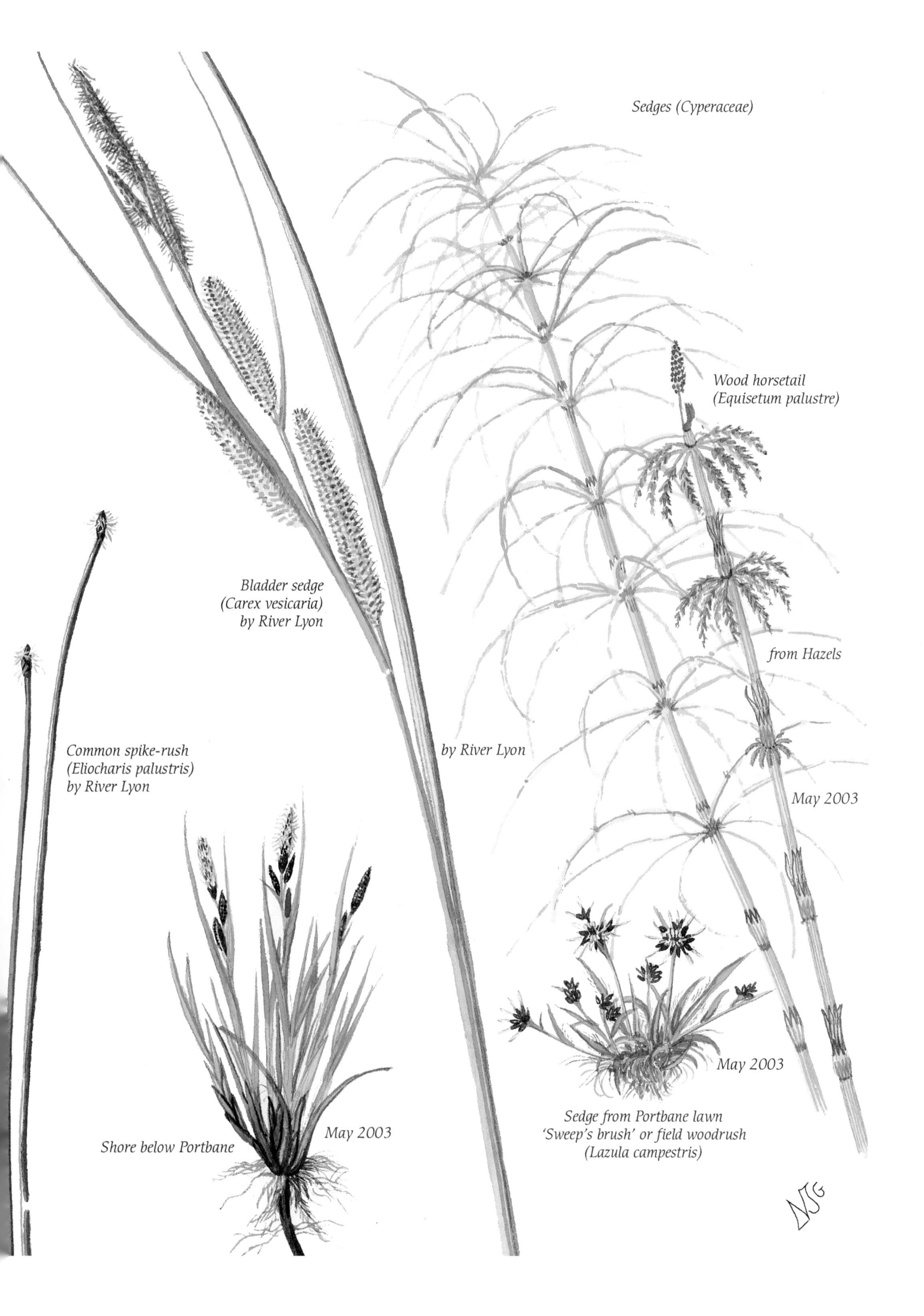
Sedges (Cyperaceae)
Wood horsetail
(Equisetum palustre)
from Hazels
May 2003
Bladder sedge
(Carex vesicaria)
by River Lyon
by River Lyon
Common spike-rush
(Eliocharis palustris)
by River Lyon
May 2003
Shore below Portbane
May 2003
Sedge from Portbane lawn
'Sweep's brush' or field woodrush
(Lazula campestris)
NJG

*Some wild flowers of late August*

*Beside Loch Tay in Summer*

*Wild Rose*

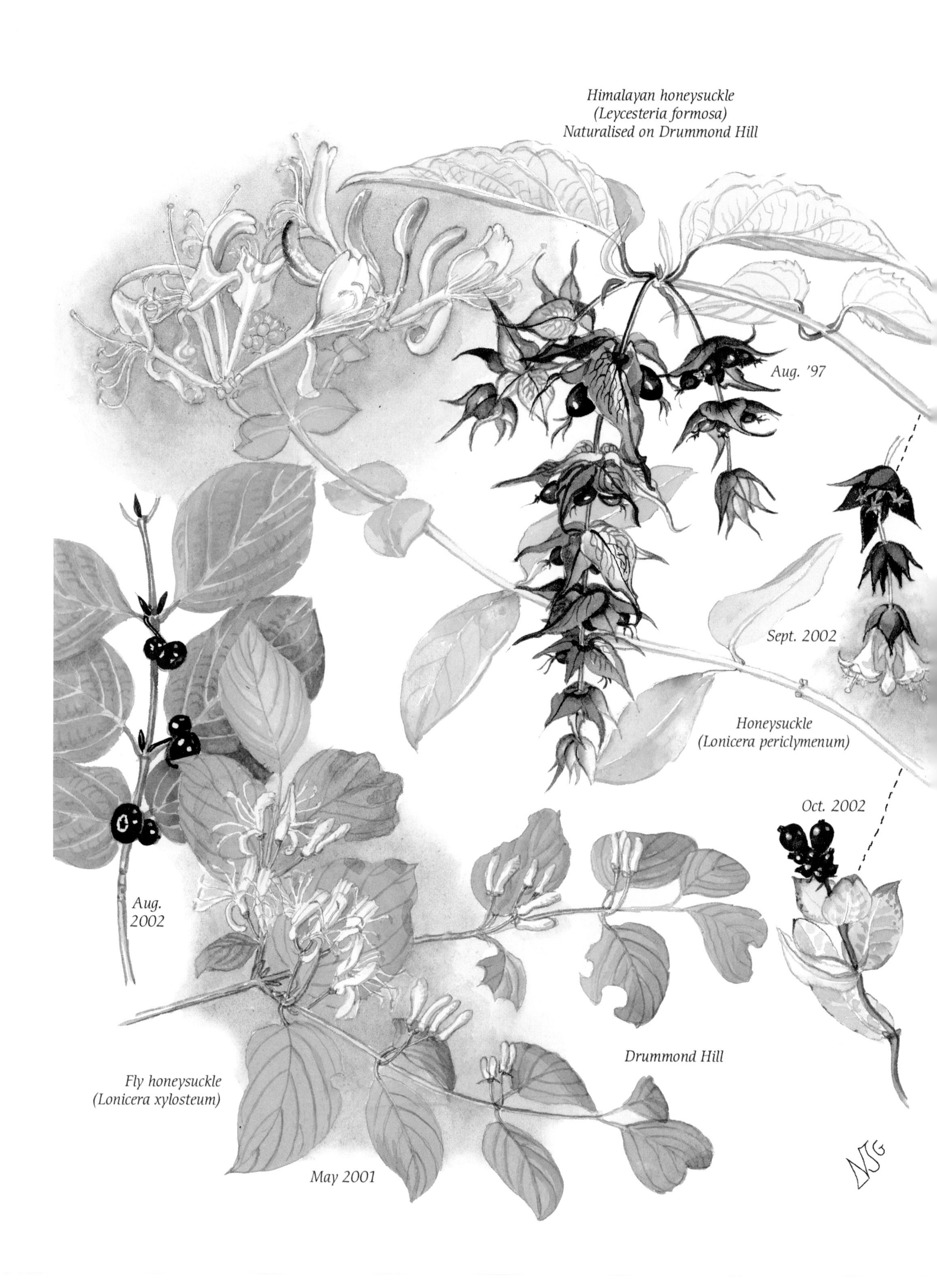
Himalayan honeysuckle
(Leycesteria formosa)
Naturalised on Drummond Hill
Aug. '97
Sept. 2002
Honeysuckle
(Lonicera periclymenum)
Oct. 2002
Aug.
2002
Drummond Hill
Fly honeysuckle
(Lonicera xylosteum)
May 2001

Mosses and Lichens

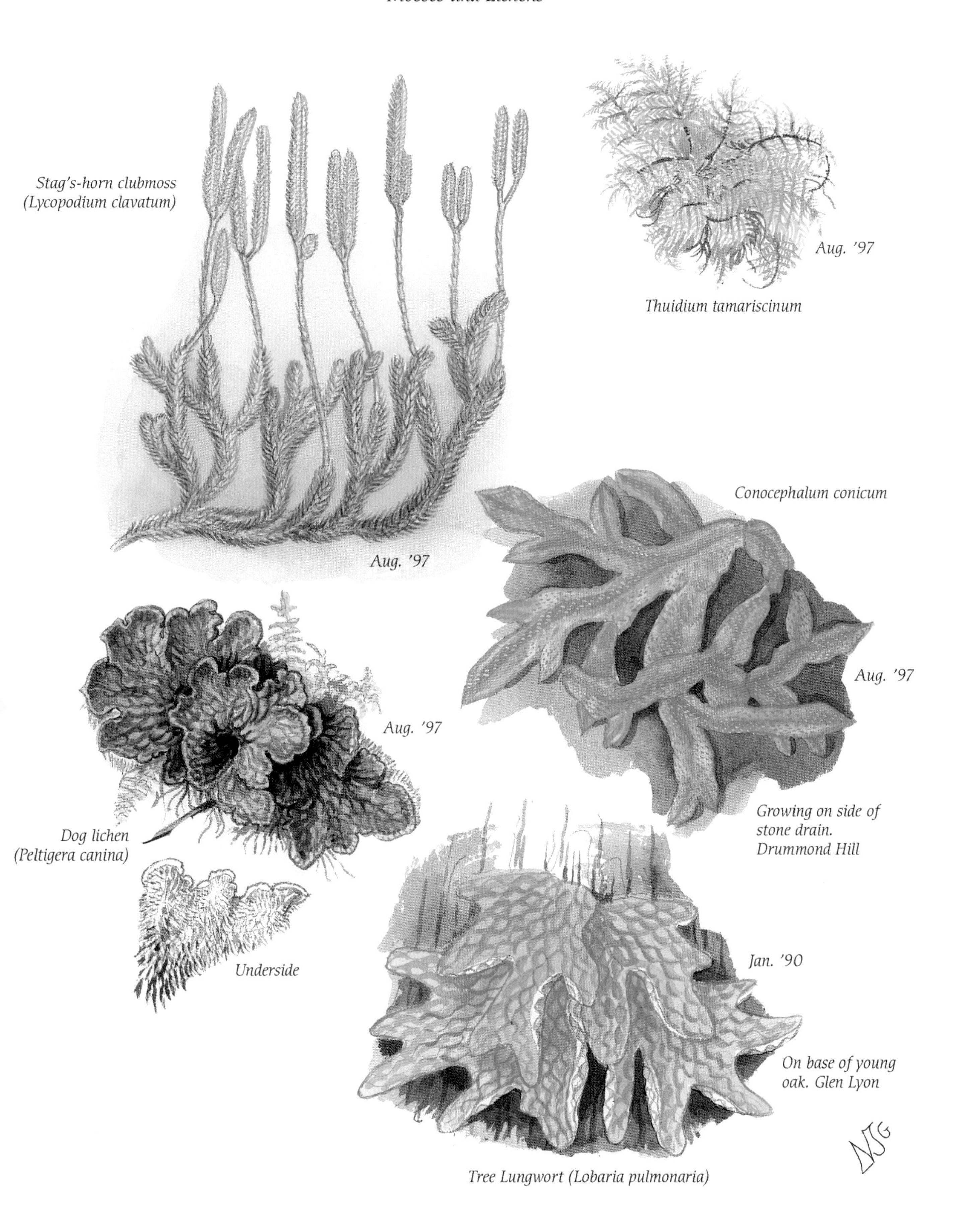

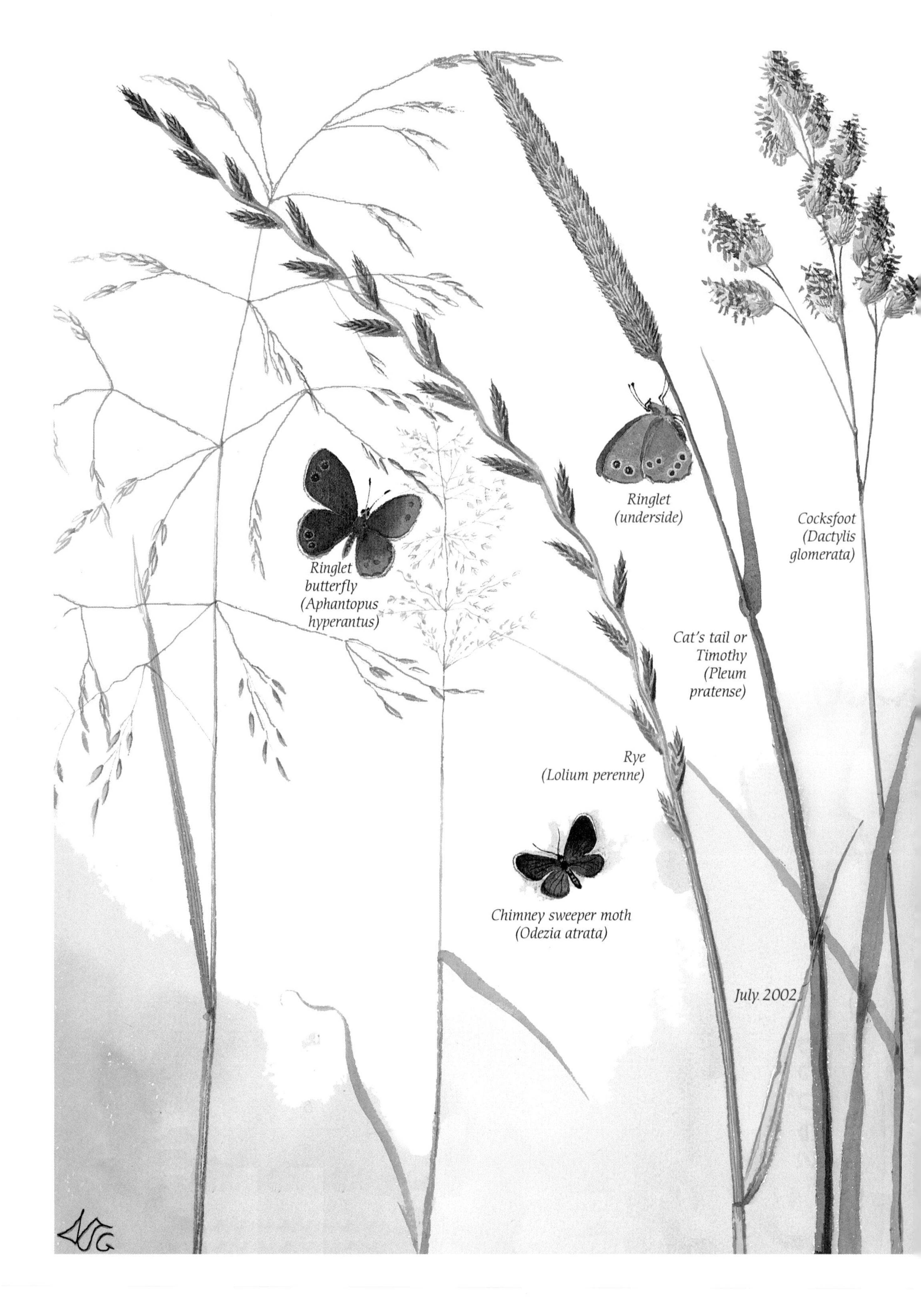
Ringlet butterfly (Aphantopus hyperantus)
Ringlet (underside)
Cocksfoot (Dactylis glomerata)
Cat's tail or Timothy (Pleum pratense)
Rye (Lolium perenne)
Chimney sweeper moth (Odezia atrata)
July 2002

Purple moor-grass
(Molinia caerulea)
Bearded twitch
(Agropyron caninum)
Woodland brome
(Bromus ramosa)
Crested dog's-tail grass
(Cynosurus cristatus)
Common blue
(Polyommatus icarus)
Aug. 2002
Small pearl-bordered fritillary
(Clossiana selene)
(Boloria selene)

*Some meadow wild flowers of September*

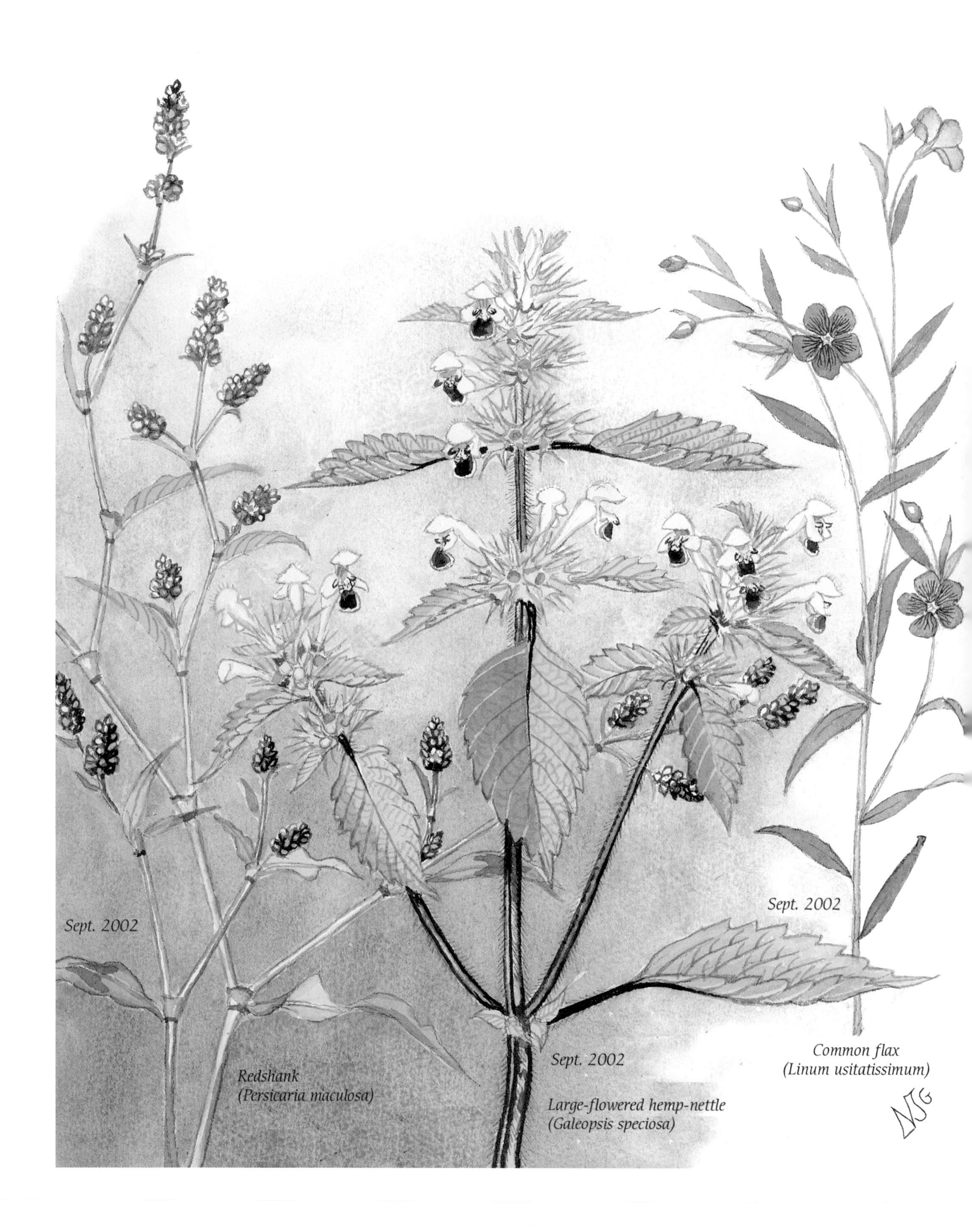

*Moths Portbane*

*Scalloped hazel*
*(Odontopera bidentata)*

*May '88*

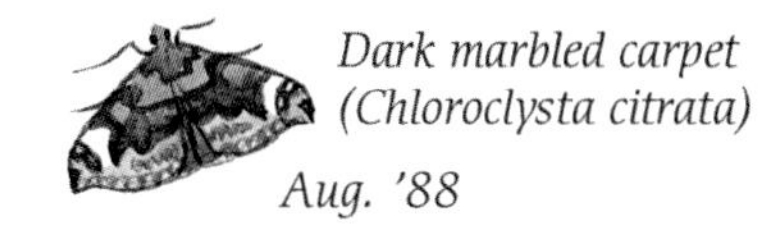

*Dark marbled carpet*
*(Chloroclysta citrata)*

*Aug. '88*

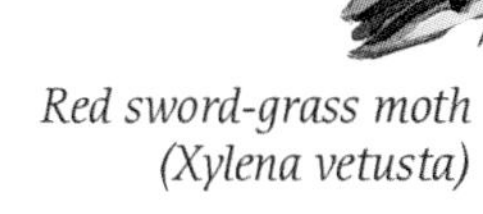

*Early thorn*
*(Selenia dentoria)*

*May '88*

*Canary-shouldered thorn*
*(Ennomos alniaria)*

*Sept. '88*

*Scarse umber*
*(Agriopis aurantiaria)*

*Nov. '84*

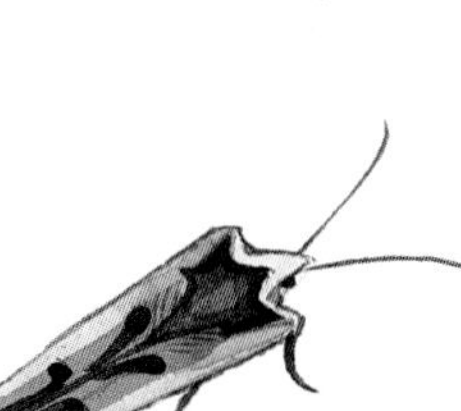

*Red sword-grass moth*
*(Xylena vetusta)*

*Sept. '88*

*Angle-shades*
*(Phlogophora meticulosa)*

*Oct. '97*

*June '68*

*Poplar hawk*
*(Laothoe populi)*

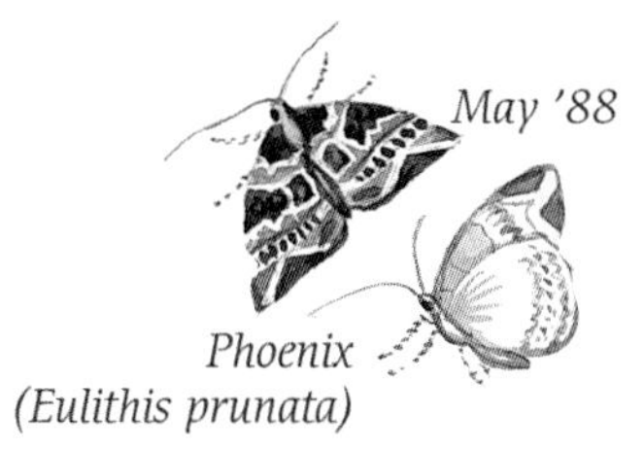

*May '88*

*Phoenix*
*(Eulithis prunata)*

*Bordered white*
*(Bupalus piniaria)*

*July '88*

*Barred red*
*(Hylaea fasciaria)*

*July '88*

*Silver-ground carpet*
*(Xanthorhoe montanata)*

*June '88*

*Greylag geese*

# Wild *geese*

Twin rhythm twines;
The quicker beating of wings
And the slow changing of lines:
Lines drawn on grey; long –
Wavering, breaking and reforming,
To the silver of goose song.

*Canada geese displaying.*
*Their necks appear very long like swans'*

Men destroyed my haven,
Walking heavy foot
With cruel thoughtless hand
Put out my fox's amber light,
All lightsome litheness gone.
Choked happiness in me
With snare-wire's bitter bite –
For what to them was work, or need;
Nor reck they of terror, pain,
Or know they sully Heaven's light
And plant of barren seed.

*Ruined cottage*

# Changes

As change is characteristic of all life, being nature's equivalent of Time, we have seen something of change by Drummond Hill in the last forty years, most or perhaps all of it instigated or assisted, often unknowingly, by man's activities and attitudes.

Almost more than anything I had always hoped to find otter sign here but although I searched in suitable places, I hardly ever found signs of their presence. Loch Tay used to be part of one of the main routes for travelling otters in the Highlands, and there were famous holts, some large enough to shelter fugitive humans, which were actually used for that purpose sometimes (in particular, one at Killin). Otters in those days were common, but due to persecution after sport fishing became popular at lodges and estates (not so much to pollution as in the south), they had become rare on inland waters in Scotland. But when it was realised that otters help keep fish-stocks healthy, and that they eat vast quantities of eels that in turn eat millions of salmon and trout eggs, protection was afforded it, and the otter is gradually recovering; for more otters mean fewer eels, which means more salmon and trout, which means more eels and more otters – but this natural equation is complicated by man's devastating effect on salmon stocks at present.

*Otter*

There is a wood we call Badger Wood (which I have not shown on the map as wicked badger-baiting is still perpetrated in Scotland) of ancient rough-trunked oaks and alders by a river where narrow paths, made by the badgers that live there, wander through the bracken. Outside the entrances to the badgers' cettes the earth is beaten smooth by the passage of many paws, and piles of discarded bedding, rotted to compost, accumulate on the river bank. In nearby meadows there are holes and snoutings made as the badgers search nocturnally for earth worms (at some times of the year their staple diet), and half-chewed bluebell bulbs can be found on the paths. A few years ago we went to the wood and searched, as we always had, for signs of otters. And there, beside water transparent as amber glass, were their tracks, impressed on a shelf of mud beneath an arching

Badger tracks

tree trunk and near to an ideal holt under old tree roots at the water's edge, and I have seen them there on each subsequent visit. Later we visited another place where I used to search hopefully but in vain; a perfect spot for otters at the confluence of two waters. Under overhanging branches and nodding melancholy thistles which sheltered a small beach of wet sand from which one could see out at surface level over the water, we found again the hand and foot prints of more than one otter visit. Not long ago I found otter spraints on rocks by the loch below our house, and otter tracks continue to be easier to find than they were. But I have still to see my first Loch Tay otter.

American mink have recently become accidentally naturalised in Britain and with few able competitors here to keep them in check they adversely affect the native fauna; especially water voles. Since the return of otters, however, the mink is said to be becoming less common, although their tracks still star the mud along many Perthshire watercourses.

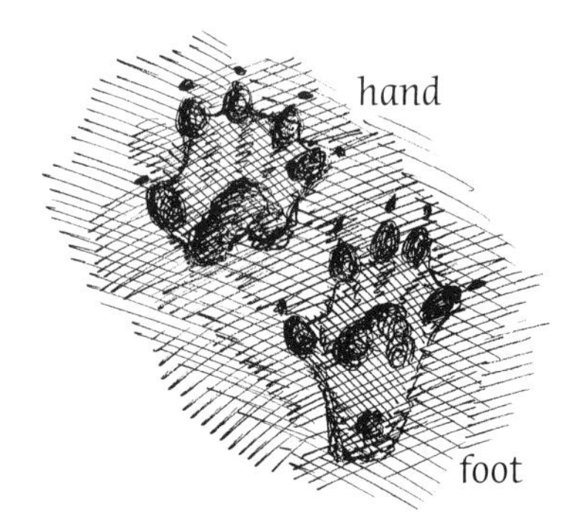

Otter tracks

Another animal that for years I hoped to find evidence of but believed we never would, was the pine marten. They had become very rare in Scotland and probably extinct in England. But shortly after we had read a description of their rowan berry-filled autumn droppings for the first time, we began to find such droppings on Drummond Hill. Over the years we found them more often, and eventually we began to see them in other places too, even on open hillsides. I had my first glimpse of a wild pine marten a few years ago as it galloped across a track, looking like a cross between a fox and a squirrel; dark auburn red with big feet and a short 'brush'. Just for a second I could not think what it was! There are places on the Hill where tufted wood-rush hides many holes and crevices in the rocks, ideal dens for martens and wildcats. It has been suggested that the pine marten may adversely effect capercaillies and red squirrels, but perhaps the increased planting of native trees, particularly Scots pines, will offset this by eventually providing a much greater area for these three creatures which previously co-existed here successfully for thousands of years. As red squirrels suffer outbreaks of disease which can decimate or even exterminate them locally, the pine marten may help prevent this by weeding out unhealthy individuals; for all predators help to keep their prey species in top condition. The grey squirrel (a naturalised Briton from America) which appears to be indirectly wiping out the

American mink

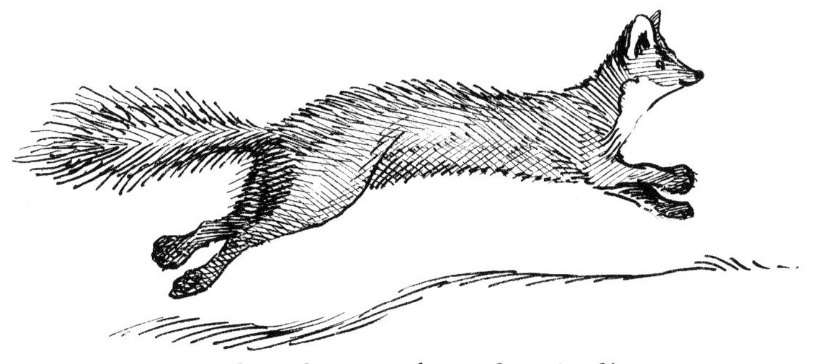
Cross between fox and squirrel!

red squirrel through a disease it carries to which the reds are susceptible, and by competition for food, has not at the time of writing (2005) yet been seen for certain in this area, although it reached Glen Almond some years ago, and has already arrived at Aberfeldy.

The marten may be a factor for crows to reckon with. Martens are said to enjoy sleeping in crows' nests and will not disdain a meal of crow's eggs or nestlings. So crows may decrease somewhat. Perhaps it will no longer be 'necessary' to build distressing crow traps on the hill in which I know buzzards have starved to death (even a golden eagle), and in one of which I recently found two ravens without water, which I released. It is a legal requirement that crow traps must be visited every day (I know that often they are not), that water must be provided at all times (it often is not) and that any other 'non targeted' bird caught must be released at once (they often are not), and that a sheltered perch must be available in the trap. The crow is a very intelligent bird which is why there are still so many of them! Drummond Hill seems to be at the border between the ranges of the ordinary black carrion crow and the hooded crow (usually considered colour varieties of the same species). Just a little to the north nearly all crows are 'hoodies' while here the 'hoodie' is unusual, although both varieties are seen together occasionally and sometimes one sees hybrids. If gamekeepers had their way and the crow disappeared, I, for one, would miss the ruffianly triple yell with which it emphatically announces its presence, and all the other things it 'says', with such a variety of notes and calls that one might almost suspect crows of having a true language, and certainly of enjoying making the sounds and varying them (they often do this even when *apparently* alone). Sound-making is particularly evident when numbers of crows are flying to roost on Drummond Hill. This applies also to the raven. Tool use was once thought to be a criterion which separated human intelligence from that of the rest of creation. But members of the crow family can not only use tools, but modify them to solve problems they have never met previously, and other animals can do the same.

*'Carrion' and 'hooded ' crows*

Before we came to Portbane fallow deer had been in the area, perhaps escaped originally from Taymouth Castle park; but I have not seen one here or met anyone who has seen one lately, although Mr Learmonth (former golf professional at Taymouth) and Duncan Menzies of Kenmore remember seeing them often before we came to the lochside. Perhaps they will return for they are common in the locality of Birnam Wood, not so far away (and possibly by Loch Rannoch). A few years ago wild boars were kept at Bolfracks but owing to official 'red tape' are sadly no longer there. However, there is a good chance that one day we may see the European beaver by Drummond Hill – home again after four or five hundred years. Nearly all European countries that once had beavers but 'lost' them, have now successfully reintroduced them – except Britain. Strangely inflexible, unimaginative and slow off the mark we sometimes seem to be.

*Fallow buck proclaiming his territory*

*Wild boar sow with piglets*

One May evening as I stood in our wood at dusk, scanning a last time with binoculars before going inside, the heads of deer appeared, silhouetted behind the fence above The Hazels. First came fifteen hinds with a small-antlered stag which milled behind the fence before beginning to jump it one by one. Others appeared until twenty-five had jumped over, but the twenty-sixth caught a foot in the wire. Finally pulling free after a struggle she cantered after the others to disappear amongst the bushes. By now many more deer were waiting to come down but the last incident seemed to have put them off the jump. I expected them to wait until it was darker, though already they were only just visible. There were about sixty red deer that evening.

*A beautiful 'head' seen in The Hazels*

From the bedroom windows of Portbane, even in summer when the deer are expected to be up on the high tops to give birth and to escape biting flies, we watched red deer in the fields in the early mornings and evenings. But they spent more time in The Hazels where I would meet them and we would stand and stare at each other before the deer turned and melted into the trees. Years later they avoided the open fields but still came off the hills by well-marked paths every evening to The Hazels, jumping the fence and tracking through the bracken on narrow paths they had made to their favourite places. In the day time we would find twigs frayed and broken by the stags where they had rubbed the velvet from their antlers in summer or thrashed the bushes during the rut in autumn. Until a few years ago they had a night 'yard' where they came during the winter to shelter in the birches near the Amulree track. Their minty scent hung warm there after they had flitted before light, and heaps of their fibrous oval droppings lay among the heavily browsed broom, gorse and blackthorn bushes. Now a large

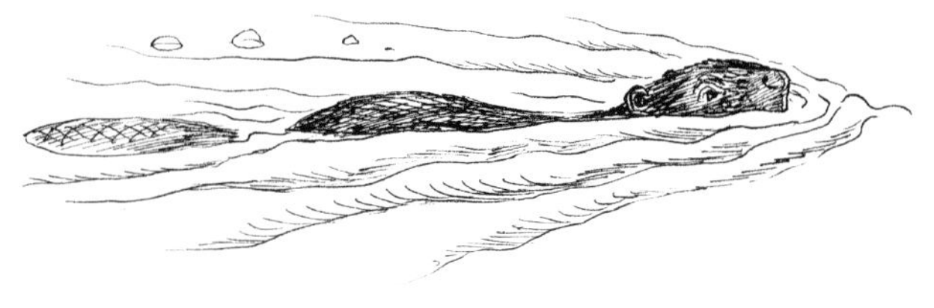

*Beaver*

*Jumping the fence*

*Weathered pine stump*

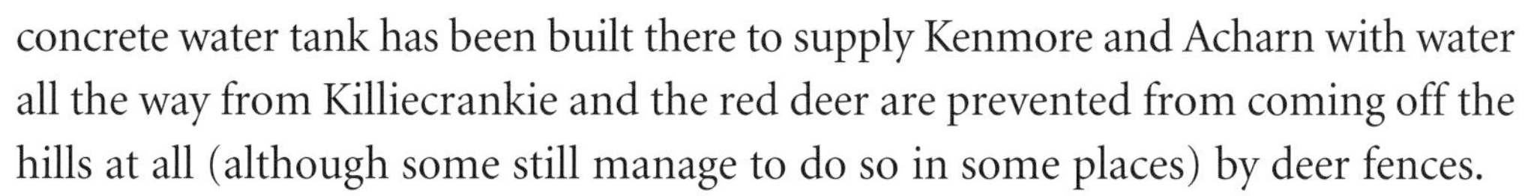

concrete water tank has been built there to supply Kenmore and Acharn with water all the way from Killiecrankie and the red deer are prevented from coming off the hills at all (although some still manage to do so in some places) by deer fences.

But although the deer are now shut out of the glens and woodlands onto the bitter uplands with little shelter or forage, where they suffer in the winter, a woodland of native trees has been re-planted on the slopes of Gunpowder Hill among the bleached stumps of Scots pines that were cut down after the First World War to make way for sheep. Even after so many years without trees it was still possible to find woodland wild flowers and plants growing on the open hillside among the stumps – wood sorrel, bitter vetch, yellow pimpernel, dog violet, wood anemone, blaeberry, bluebells, and stag's horn clubmoss – and on some hillsides, chickweed winter-green. Already the trees of this new wood on Gunpowder Hill stand out above the skyline like feathered Tin-tin Red Indian warriors, taller each year, where one had thought that trees would never grow again because of the sheep (also now fenced out), and junipers have re-sprung from stems previously eaten to the ground while others have been planted. So the fence, if not beneficial to deer, is so to trees. Hundreds of new birchlings, rowans, oaklets and Scots pinelings have sprouted in Curlew Wood of their own volition under parent trees which had grown old without offspring, and thousands of other native trees have been planted out. Already the young rowans are bearing berries which will feed more fieldfares, mistle thrushes and redwings (and perhaps young pine martens) in autumn and winter months to come. How much richer this wood will be than the usual commercial plantation put heartlessly on the side of a hill like black, geometrical graffiti.

*Chickweed-wintergreen*

The Hazels above Portbane are now also fenced as an area of natural interest. Sheep which for so long had prevented regeneration have been removed. The old hazels, birches, hawthorns and blackthorns are putting out new shoots, and seedlings and saplings have come up. The longer grasses have encouraged a variety of moths such as the little charcoal-grey chimney sweep, and the black spot which swings to and fro as if on a thread, a blurred orange arc in the air, before settling. In some years ringlet butterflies can be seen in June by the hundred where, before, one would have been lucky to see even one.

*Blackface sheep*

*Blackface ram*

It would perhaps be a mistake to believe, as some people do, that sheep are only destructive. There are hillside meadows and banks so shortly grazed by them that the tiniest wild flowers have a chance to grow, and if their grazing is managed they can be a useful tool for conservation; And what could be better than hill-fed roast mutton with rowan or redcurrant jelly? The Scottish blackface sheep is a useful and attractive animal; it produces good wool as well as mutton. But diversity and moderation are keys to natural richness in the landscape, and ultimately probably to the healthy productivity of the land.

How light the bones, antlers and skulls of wild Scottish red deer have become, owing to lack of woodland browse and the minerals obtainable from it. Two skulls found in The Hazels shortly before deer were fenced out (of an old hind and a young stag) were almost paper thin and much lighter than the skulls of similar-sized animals that we find in Africa. Red deer in present conditions might one day become a miniature and horn-less race in Scotland. Antlers of many stags shot not long ago before so many woods were either cut down, fenced or died out, were larger than anything a wild-living Scottish stag normally produces today: great candelabra with thickly beaded peat-brown branches tipped with many ivory tines. But the deer are magnificent even so. The sound of their roaring in the rut in October carries to our house from a long way off on the frosty air as a vibration at the extremity of hearing, felt rather than heard; or loud from Drummond Hill where a few stags may have escaped the oft-repeated culls there. It sounds something like the bellowing of hungry stirks but with a wild, gut-racking quality that the voices of cattle do not have; although the ringing, repeated bellow of a short-horn bull is magnificent too in its way – an echo of aurochs of old. Cattle seem at home in the woods and there is something satisfying in seeing them there. Although they can be the gentlest and friendliest of animals, they have never lost a latent wildness that comes out when they have been unattended for a while, and perhaps if left to themselves it would not take them long to return entirely to the wild (as blackfaced sheep have done in some places locally). It would need the predatory attention of the wolf, however, to transform modern cattle to the magnificence of their Aurochs ancestors.

*Old magnificence*

*Aurochs*

Noticeable changes have occurred in bird life over the last 30 years. It seemed there were no green woodpeckers as far north as Loch Tay when we came to Portbane (although they had been recorded up until 1895 in Glengarry, when they disappeared) and were described in 1938 as rare vagrants to Scotland, but in July 1968 I heard a yaffling call near Perth. It was not until 1988 that we heard one on Drummond Hill (although they may well have arrived earlier), and a few days later saw a green woodpecker in the field behind Portbane, swooping down and up in its flight as telegraph wires swoop beside a moving train. Later I found a green wing feather in the grounds of Taymouth Castle. So the yaffle had already arrived and is now seen and heard here nearly as often as the greater spotted woodpecker – itself fully recovered since the Second World War.

*Turtle dove*

Another bird that was not here until fairly recently, and was not native to Britain at all, but which has been moving steadily northwards until it has colonised almost every area, is the collared dove: whereas the native stock dove and turtle dove have both declined, the latter almost disappearing (I have seen only three turtle doves here in many visits over thirty five years). Stock doves were persecuted along with wood pigeons which are still often shot, but must have been less resilient than the latter bird which still exists in good numbers. Perhaps they are more dependent on grain fields than the wood pigeon. But collared doves prefer the vicinity of houses and gardens.

House sparrows by Drummond Hill were once more common than they have lately become, being at one time the commonest, or at any rate the most familiar, of all small birds around houses. (But while they decline in Britain, the Indian race of the house sparrow is steadily and successfully colonising East Africa, arriving in our Kenya farmyard in 2000). Sparrows used to nest at Portbane, and often came into the house to help themselves to crumbs, or to peck at cold potatoes or other food in the kitchen. We loved their sleepy 'chip-chip' calls, somehow redolent of summertime and peace. (Once we saw a buzzard plucking a sparrow it had killed outside our front door. When it had finished, the sparrow was as neatly prepared as a bought chicken ready for cooking). For thirty years sparrows deserted Portbane, for there are no small grain fields nearby, fewer wild weed-seeds for food, and fewer suitable nesting cavities anywhere. But do these reasons explain why sparrows are also disappearing from London where they used to be so common? Perhaps there is a serious shortage of nesting material in the metropolis and horses are no longer fed from nosebags in the streets there. Occasionally a sparrow would join the other birds at the food we put out for them in winter, on its way between Acharn and Kenmore, where house sparrows still live, and in the Spring last year a pair built a nest under the eaves of Portbane and we are hoping for a sparrow renaissance. The chaffinch seems to be the most common small seed-eater in this part of Scotland. They sometimes gather in large flocks in the winter months, their numbers swelled by continental immigrants which often include a few bramblings. Siskins, as mentioned previously, have

*House sparrows*

*Dotterel*

greatly increased, while corn buntings which we used often to see, are now almost non-existent around Loch Tay, and yellowhammers are no longer common. Starlings, too, seem to be steadily disappearing just as the sparrow has done – probably for the same reasons.

The dotterel, a mountain bird, is said to be disappearing from the Glen Lyon hills where it used to be quite common. Is this because of disturbance by hill walkers (unlikely as nearly all 'Munro' climbers stick to the paths) or to do with a change in the climate, or to some other cause?

One of the most noticeable of man-wrought changes is the dearth of skylarks in agricultural country and moorland where they used to be common; although there are still many meadow pipits on the hills which steeple into the air singing, to parachute down above their nests under tussocks where females may be sitting on glossy, olive eggs. And now and again there is still to be heard out of the blue the joyful 'twiddling' song of a skylark to show what we are missing – one of the happiest sounds I know.

*Goshawk on pheasant*

Golden-eye ducks may be breeding in our area sometimes now, an occurrence that used to be rare, for we see pairs here during their late nesting season. Canada geese, comparatively new to Britain as a wild bird, have nested in the kind of wild and marshy country in which greylags used to nest. Greylag geese bred all over England and Scotland once upon a time but were eventually hounded out by shooters, trappers, egg-takers, changes in agriculture, and the draining of marshes. Perhaps one day they will breed here again (perhaps are doing so already) as they have started to do in other parts of Scotland, instead of migrating to Iceland. Recently I saw a pair of scaup on the loch in August and wondered if they also had bred here.

The buzzard has increased owing to legal protection, while it seems to me that the kestrel has declined. Buzzards, which normally mate for life, can live for over twenty years in the wild.

*Red kite*

Very exciting is the return of the osprey which is often seen flying spiderishy over Loch Tay, perching on big trees by the waterside or catching pike in Kenmore bay. And herein lies another natural equation which illustrates how predators play a useful role in natural productivity. Pike eat ducklings, but ospreys mean fewer pike, which means more ducks; and more ducks mean more pike, which means more ospreys, which means more ducks etc. One recent spring I thought I saw my first red kite (still in danger of illegal poisoning in Scotland although they are harmless from a 'gamekeeping' point of view) from the top of Drummond Hill, and in March 2004 I had a very good view of one by the Duneaves road. But perhaps most exciting of all to watch are the local peregrines which somehow managed to survive here always, even in those depressing years in the nineteen sixties and seventies of DDT poisoning, and in spite of persecution. Two years ago I watched a pair, bright against a background of forest and cliff, as the falcon flew up in broad tacks then turned and slid on a diagonal, faster and faster, tipped suddenly and plummeted like a stone towards the tiercel: then up again like a ball bounced hard. They did this alternately, calling harshly to each other, and between-whiles they cruised fast and level, to and fro against the hillside. Sometimes peregrines enjoy harassing other birds of prey. They make 'squeeze-bottle' call notes and a whinnying chitter, as well as a harsh chatter, to be heard ringing imperiously over hill and wood. Sadly, they are still harassed here by egg-collectors and by the kidnapping and lucrative sale of young birds from the eyrie, to falconers. Sea eagles are very occasionally seen over Loch Tay and perhaps soon Loch Earn (not far away) will be earning its name again – 'Earn' being the old name for sea eagle.

*Peregrine harassing buzzard*

Sparrowhawks, also rare not so long ago through DDT poisoning and persecution, are often in evidence although they and the kestrel are still subject to alarming local 'disappearances'. Even the gosshawk is back to breed in certain forest plantations. I saw one standing on the body of a black pheasant in such a plantation near the roadside.

Perhaps one day soon, with more sympathetic and varied farming practices, the corncrake will return to Loch Tayside. The only water-rail I have ever seen here was crossing the road to a field pond by Drummond Hill in 1969.

*Corncrake*

Freshwater mussels are to be found in the Tay and the Lyon, and travelling tinsmith families used to 'farm' them for the beautiful pearls they sometimes contain. These families had traditional 'fishing' grounds where the mussel shells were carefully levered open a little way, inspected for pearls, sometimes numbered, and returned unharmed to the river to continue growing; for freshwater mussels can live to be over one hundred years old and might produce more than one pearl. But later, ignorant gangs and greedy individuals took over the 'fishing', slashing open the mussels ruthlessly, even very small ones, and leaving heaps of them dead and useless on the banks, until the mussels have become rare and the 'industry' is no longer sustainable. Now, theoretically, there are fines of thousands of pounds for those caught so much as disturbing a freshwater mussel although I still find heaps of mussel shells that have been slashed open. Perhaps one day the molluscs will recover so that pearl fishing may be practised properly again.

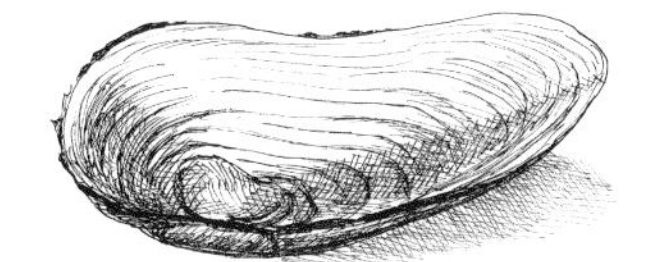

*Freshwater mussel*

The most obvious changes we have seen have been in agriculture, and this, of course, has affected wild life greatly. When my brother and I first began to come to Loch Tay as children with our parents, and later in the summer holidays from school when my father fished for brown trout in Loch Tay, we stayed at the Ardeonaig Hotel. It was a simple, country hotel then, and the whitewashed farm buildings around it, once stabling for horses and carriages, were full of martin's, swallow's and sparrow's nests. The track opposite the hotel that follows the big Ardeonaig burn up the hill was unsurfaced and banked on either hand with a profusion of wild flowers: meadow cranesbill, hedge woundwart, tufted vetch,

*Fishing weather*

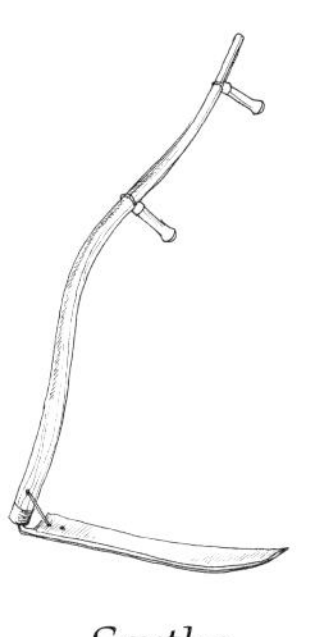

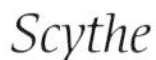

*Scythe*

*Harrowing above Loch Tay*

*Cocked oats*

*Hay stooks*

*Lift in pony cart*

yellow archangel, harebell, bladder campion, lady's bedstraw, orchises and many others. Small fields of oats and hay on the hillsides were still cut by hand with scythes, the hay piled into small silvery stooks with pitchforks, and the grain cocked up in sheaves by hand. There were still a few Clydesdale horses for the ploughing on the lochside. This was about 50 years ago, and less. Since then, small cultivated fields have dwindled and more and more sheep have taken over the low fields and the open hill. In the more fertile spots, silage is now grown and stuffed into giant 'dinosaur eggs' of black polythene, while hay is stored in rolls so large that they can be moved only by huge earth-compacting machines too large for the local roads. These changes were driven by unwise agricultural policy and subsidies, and things will change again with recent improvements in policy and grants. But many of the country people who were farming when we were very young have gone, and many of the tumbled down crofts and small stone houses in which they lived have been replaced with smart holiday homes empty for much of the year.

So changes happen fast amongst people too. Bessy MacDonald, who always sat in the pew behind us in the Kirk of Kenmore, lived at Portbane Farm in the fields behind our house, after her marriage until her husband retired from farming. Yet over thirty years ago the farmhouse was already a ruin – just a few large grey stones to show where once it had stood, and an outbuilding with an open space where the track leads into what had once been the farm yard. Mrs MacDonald was still middle-aged then, but little remained of her former home. As a girl she took a position as a maid at Remony House and at Portbane, long before we came. The staff were expected to behave with decorum and be in bed early. But Bessy would climb out of her window at Remony and walk to Ardeonaig by moonlight to attend dances at the hotel (there were very few cars at that time and the road was unsurfaced). Then she would walk home again in the early hours and climb in through her window: a round trip of about twelve miles with hours of dancing between.

Ruby MacGreggor used to come twice a week without fail, for twenty years, to help my parents in the house. She was brought up at a village called Styx, or Stix, near the pre-historic stone circle of Croft Morag, a village which was originally built in 1800 for employees of Lord Breadalbane. She remembered as a child walking barefoot from there even in snow and ice, to school at Acharn every morning (although there was actually a school at Stix too), then walking home again in the afternoon, although sometimes they got a lift with a pony and cart. This was a total distance of some five miles. Yet long before we came to Loch Tay, Stix, too, was a ruin of broken-down, window-pierced stone walls in the fields under the old trees. Now there is talk of rebuilding there.

Ruby's husband, Alec MacGreggor, a forester who worked on Drummond Hill, used to help us in the garden at Portbane. He was very strong and I remember seeing him pick up a tree he had just finished cutting through with his axe, while it still stood upright, and walking with it so that it would fall in a better place when he put it down. This tree had a trunk at least a foot in diameter and was perhaps forty feet tall. I used to question Mr MacGreggor about the forest on Drummond Hill. He said there were no pine martens there at all then (late 1960s), and we never found any signs of them either, at that time. He occasionally saw Scottish wildcats but he said these were always shot if possible. I asked if the cats came off Drummond Hill to maraud. He said that they did not but that they did a lot of killing on the hill, particularly of rabbits, mice and voles – sometimes young roe deer. I wondered then why it was thought necessary by the Forestry Commission to kill the cats at all, as they could not have been detrimental to forestry in any way – on the contrary. A few years ago my daughter Laria, and her fiancé, had a good view of a wildcat as it walked along the top of a mossy wall on Drummond Hill. And I glimpsed one at the top of the fields behind Portbane. They are no longer very rare in Scotland but may inter-breed with feral domestic cats and are still sometimes illegally persecuted, and caught in snares set for foxes. My painting was done from sketches of a pair of tame wildcats belonging to Mr Terry Nutkins, many years ago.

*Fleeting glimpse (Wildcat)*

One day I found a tin containing some substance on the wall in Portbane garden and took a sniff at it. Mystified, I carried the tin to the house to ask about it. It was cyanide, used by Mr MacGreggor to poison wasps in their bikes in the ground. He would scoop it from the tin with the nail of his little finger, specially grown for the job, and put it into the entrance to the bikes; a highly risky activity, not only to wasps! I think he also used it to poison moles (though not in our garden). Moles are even now sometimes poisoned or trapped in the fields; I once saw a line of 15 dead moles hung on a fence on a neighbouring estate. Yet their activities are beneficial to land, turning and aerating soil which becomes compacted, especially where heavy tractors have lumbered over it. Moles sometimes worry tidy gardeners, but if molehills on lawns are raked, spreading the earth over the grass, this will encourage fresh grass to grow, and discourage moss. The old and seemingly ingrained attitude of killing by any means almost everything that isn't

*Tragic gibbet of innocent moles*

*Snare set in underpass of old stone wall*

'game' (and then killing the game too) must surely be changing from 'inside' with better understanding of ecology, and by a more creative and flexible attitude towards making a living in the country.

Mr Harkness who lived at his farm, Balmacnaughton, on the Queen's Drive above Remony homestead, and used to come down in earlier days to collect supplies with a horse-drawn 'sledge', helped in the garden at Portghlas next to Portbane. Mr Harkness was a true, old-fashioned country man, and we admired him and were fond of him. But I remember being upset when I discovered he had caught a hedgehog in a trap he had set for a rabbit (and about which he had asked my father 'not to tell the lassie'). Traps were widespread then and I quite often came upon gin-traps and other spring-traps set in the hedgerows. They were still legal in those days. Kelso was caught in a gin that had been set in a line of others along a field edge to catch pheasants. Corn had been scattered about each trap. A gin would break the legs of a pheasant and it was a terribly cruel way to catch them; quite apart from the fact that the person who had set the traps was not the 'owner' of the pheasants. Kelso was shocked enough to bite my hand as I opened the trap to free him. On another occasion my thumb was flattened while un-setting such a trap. Gin traps are now illegal, but the snare, perhaps even more cruel, is still allowed, although in spite of 'guidelines', it is impossible to use them humanely. For this reason I am convinced they too must soon be made illegal.

*A wooden caravan*

Dochy and his wife Rachel, a golden-haired virago, and their three daughters, were tinsmiths who lived on the lochside under the road bank in a small wooden caravan, near Croft na Caber which was a private house in those days. The three little girls, wild and pretty as briar roses with their pink complexions, grey eyes and tawny, tangled hair, would come shyly to ask my mother to alter or mend clothes for the family. Their attractive pronunciation of words led sometimes to an *impasse* in communications; for instance, when they asked if we had any spare 'squeeze'. It took my mother a while to discover that they meant 'squares', and were hoping for head-squares. Another time there was a puzzling conversation about 'jewks', which turned out to be 'ducks'. Sometimes my one-legged, ex-army father was asked by Rachel or Dochy to sort out noisy 'ruckuses' when too much drink had been taken (often when Mrs Dochy's relatives were camped nearby). Occasionally Kelso went as 'back up' for he was impressive when growling at the end of his lead. But Dochy himself was a quiet-spoken and gentle man. Tall and thin, he had been consumptive, and lived on a small army pension and social benefits. Nearly every day he would bicycle with his tin can to the Holy well at the corner beyond Portbane, to collect water for his family. If we met him on the road he would get off his bicycle to quietly pass the time of day. Dochy kept the well, little more than a field drain bubbling into a small, rocky basin, surrounded by kingcups and brooklime in spring, free of mud and dead leaves. Long ago, nuns from a nunnery on Queen Sybilla's island at the end of the loch would row over

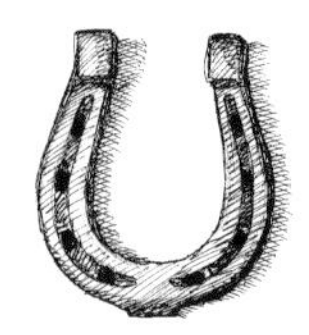

*Old shoe for a Clydesdale (hind foot)*

to Portbane* in order to collect water from this well, which was believed to have curative properties (particularly good for whooping cough). Once my mother thought she saw a group of nuns in brown habits by the well, but as she drew near, she found they were tree trunks. Now the well is forgotten and choked with leaves and mud.

Dochy used to earn pennies in Kenmore on holidays by playing the pipes. He was to have played at our wedding reception in the garden at Portbane, but the policeman who was kindly organising the parking of cars in a field near the caravan, knowing nothing of the arrangement, prevented Dochy walking up. This is something I still regret. Dochy and his wife are no longer alive but we heard that their three pretty daughters married well. There is now nothing to show that anyone once lived in the wood on the lochshore except for some daffodils in the hedge-bank planted by Dochy himself. Recently I found a china button there, with four holes in it. And we had a little cat, born under the potting-shed at Portbane, daughter of a feral cat believed to be descended from ones that Dochy kept. She lived with us in Kenya and was called 'Tay Puttle'.

*Daffodils*

How Rachel managed to keep her family even reasonably clean, healthy and sane in such a tiny dwelling, without running water or sanitation, was a miracle that must redound to her credit.

---

There is one change I for one would be very happy to see in the countryside. As hunting, shooting and fishing are still important to some people, they can very well be done in a way that is not damaging to 'ecosystems'. In this context surely *driven* shoots are not only out of date, but unsustainable; just as large-scale trawling with its accidental bycatch of cetations and unwanted fish species is unsustainable. The production of high 'surplus' numbers of pheasants and grouse has been paid for by a ruthless persecution of wild predators now and in the recent past. The argument that, if predators were allowed to increase without 'control' there would be no game birds or other animals, does not hold water. On our ranch in Kenya we are lucky enough to have still all the naturally occurring predators – lions, leopards, cheetahs, caracals, servals, wildcats, genets, civets, foxes, hyenas, jackals, painted wild-dogs, otters, mongooses, zorillas, ratels, snakes, monitor lizards, many species of eagles, hawks, falcons, buzzards, ravens and owls (including eagle owls) – yet game birds and all other 'prey' animals are very numerous, and we do not 'control' any predator. However, the population of game birds would not be sustainable if we were to do driven shoots. The shooting of a few brace by walking up *is* sustainable, and could be done often, without making a serious dent in populations.

*Tay Puttle*

In Scotland the hills are often diversified to increase their profitability to grouse in particular, by burning patches of heather: the more small areas of

*Portbane probably means 'white port', for there was a lime kiln down by the shore here, the remains of which could be seen until recently – but it could derive from 'port of the women' for *ban* means both 'white' and 'women' in Gaelic.

*Golden eagle with eaglet*

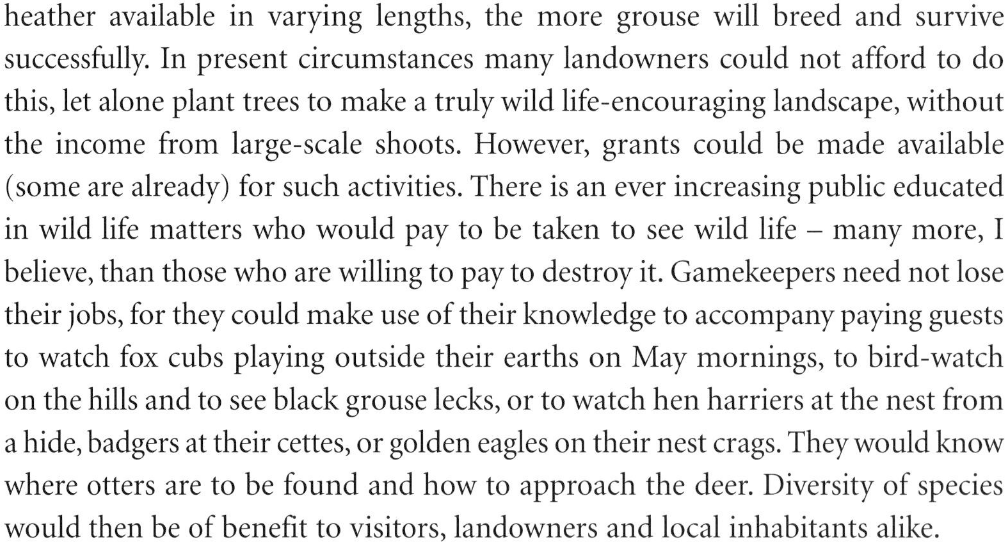

heather available in varying lengths, the more grouse will breed and survive successfully. In present circumstances many landowners could not afford to do this, let alone plant trees to make a truly wild life-encouraging landscape, without the income from large-scale shoots. However, grants could be made available (some are already) for such activities. There is an ever increasing public educated in wild life matters who would pay to be taken to see wild life – many more, I believe, than those who are willing to pay to destroy it. Gamekeepers need not lose their jobs, for they could make use of their knowledge to accompany paying guests to watch fox cubs playing outside their earths on May mornings, to bird-watch on the hills and to see black grouse lecks, or to watch hen harriers at the nest from a hide, badgers at their cettes, or golden eagles on their nest crags. They would know where otters are to be found and how to approach the deer. Diversity of species would then be of benefit to visitors, landowners and local inhabitants alike.

To illustrate how rich the fauna of Scotland was before the fashion for driven bird shoots, here is a list of 'vermin' killed in Glen Garry when such shoots began during the years 1837–1840, which shows how many predators the Scottish Highlands could support before they (the predators) were virtually – and in some cases completely – wiped out in 'sporting' interests. It must be remembered that Glen Garry also held a considerable human population (decimated at the same time as the 'vermin' purge by the Highland Clearances).

*Eagle owl*

Killed in 1837–1840 Glen Garry

| | | | |
|---|---|---|---|
| 11 | foxes | 5 | Marsh harriers |
| 198 | Wild cats | 63 | Gosshawks |
| 246 | Martin cats | 285 | Common buzzards |
| 106 | Pole cats | 3 | honey buzzards |
| 301 | stoats and weasels | 462 | kestrels |
| 67 | badgers | 78 | Merlin hawks |
| 48 | otters | 63 | Hen harriers |
| 78 | House cats (going wild) | 6 | Jer falcons |
| 27 | White tailed sea eagles | 9 | Ash-coloured or longtailed hawks |
| 15 | Golden eagles | 1431 | Hoodie crows |
| 18 | Ospreys | 475 | Ravens |
| 98 | Blue hawks | 35 | Horned owls |
| 7 | Orange-legged falcons | 71 | fern owls |
| 11 | Hobby hawks | 3 | Golden owls |
| 275 | kites or salmon-tailed gleds | 8 | Magpies |

Spelling and nomenclature as in original list, published in *Placenames of Glengarry and Glenquoich* by Edward C. Ellice – first published 1898.

*Dochy's holy well*
*May 2000*

*Old birches in the Manse glebe, September*

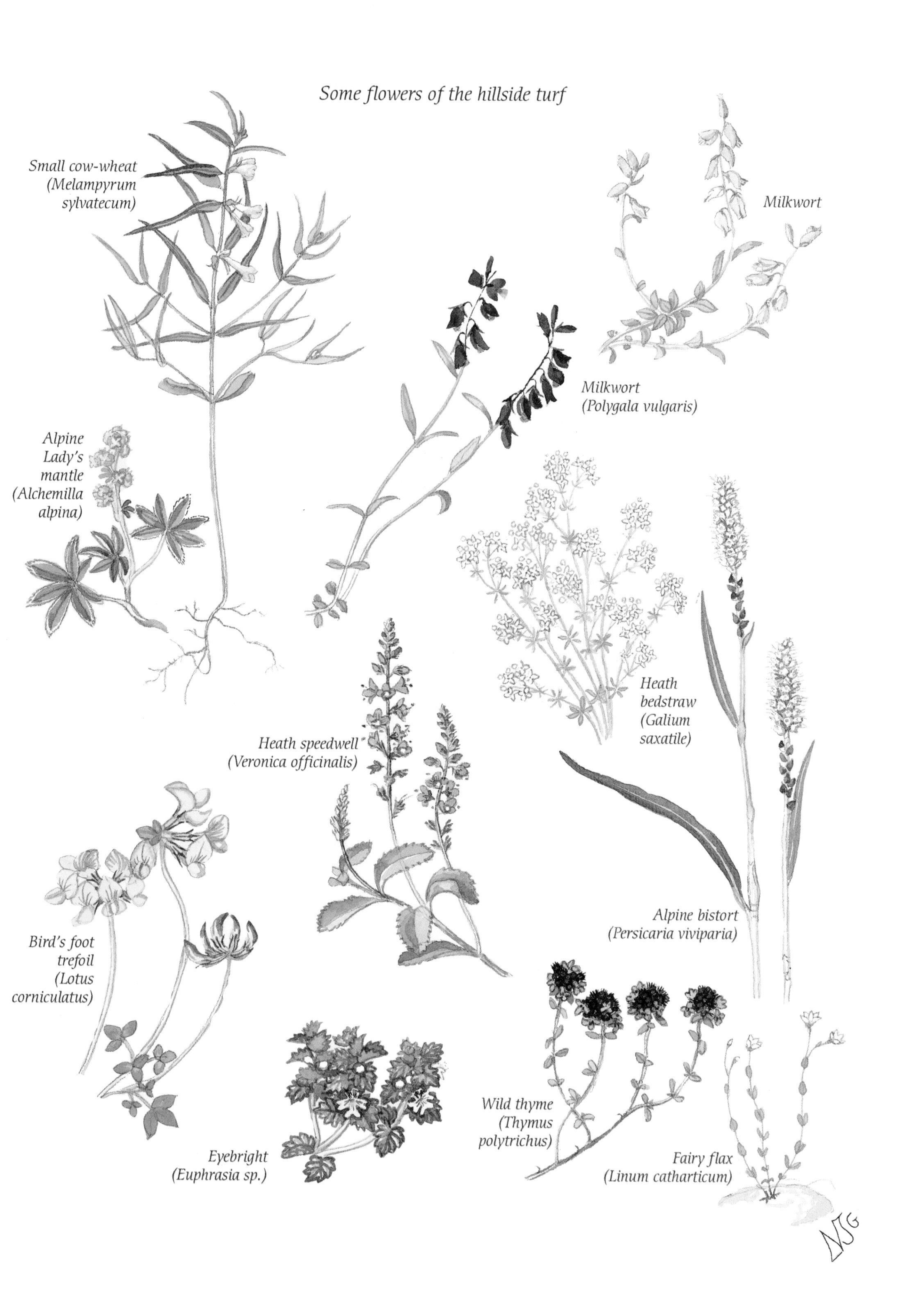
Some flowers of the hillside turf
Small cow-wheat
(Melampyrum
sylvatecum)
Milkwort
Milkwort
(Polygala vulgaris)
Alpine
Lady's
mantle
(Alchemilla
alpina)
Heath
bedstraw
(Galium
saxatile)
Heath speedwell
(Veronica officinalis)
Alpine bistort
(Persicaria vivipara)
Bird's foot
trefoil
(Lotus
corniculatus)
Wild thyme
(Thymus
polytrichus)
Eyebright
(Euphrasia sp.)
Fairy flax
(Linum catharticum)

*Badgers in Badger wood*
*(Sketches from memory)*

*Some plants that indicate old woodland when found in open*

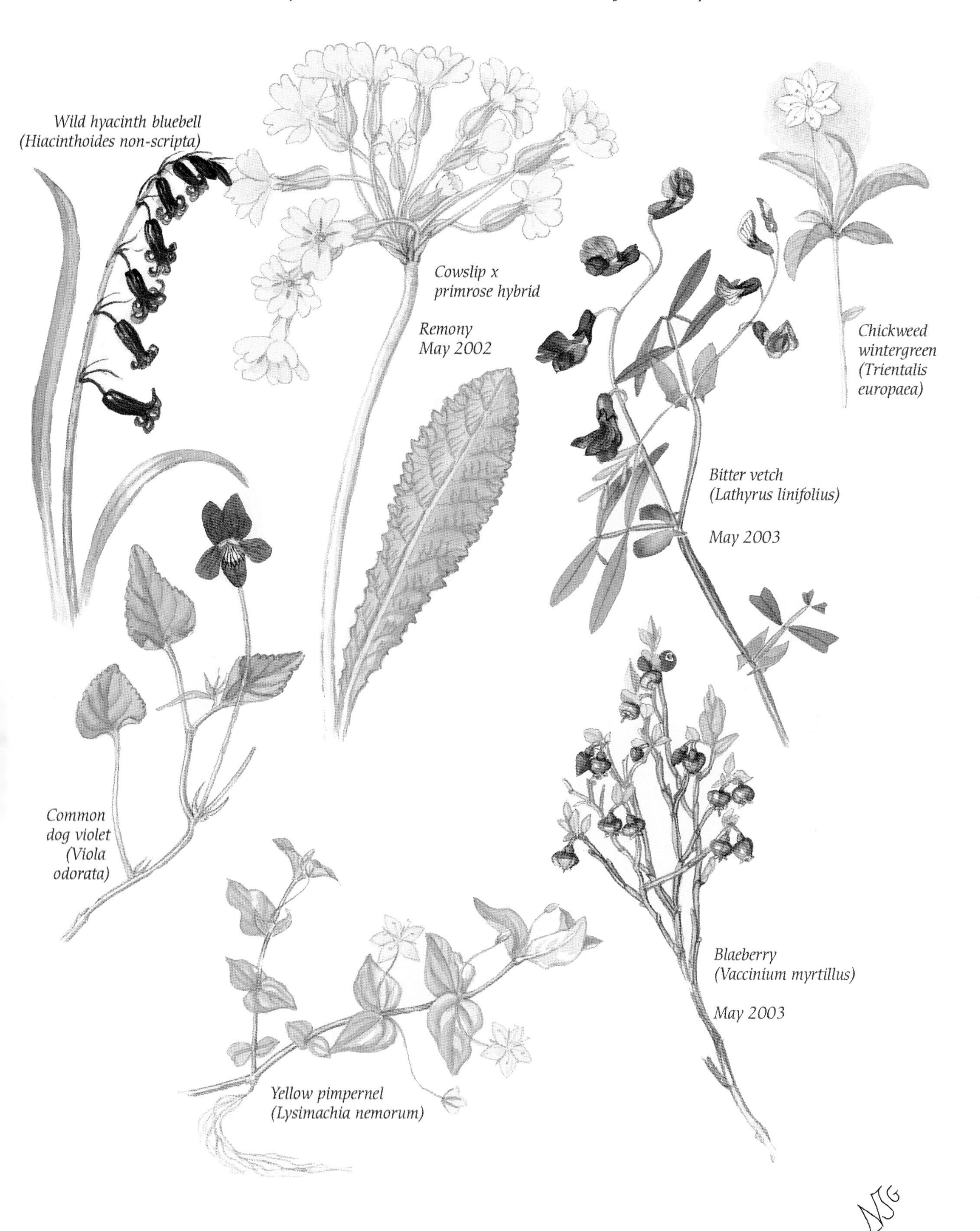

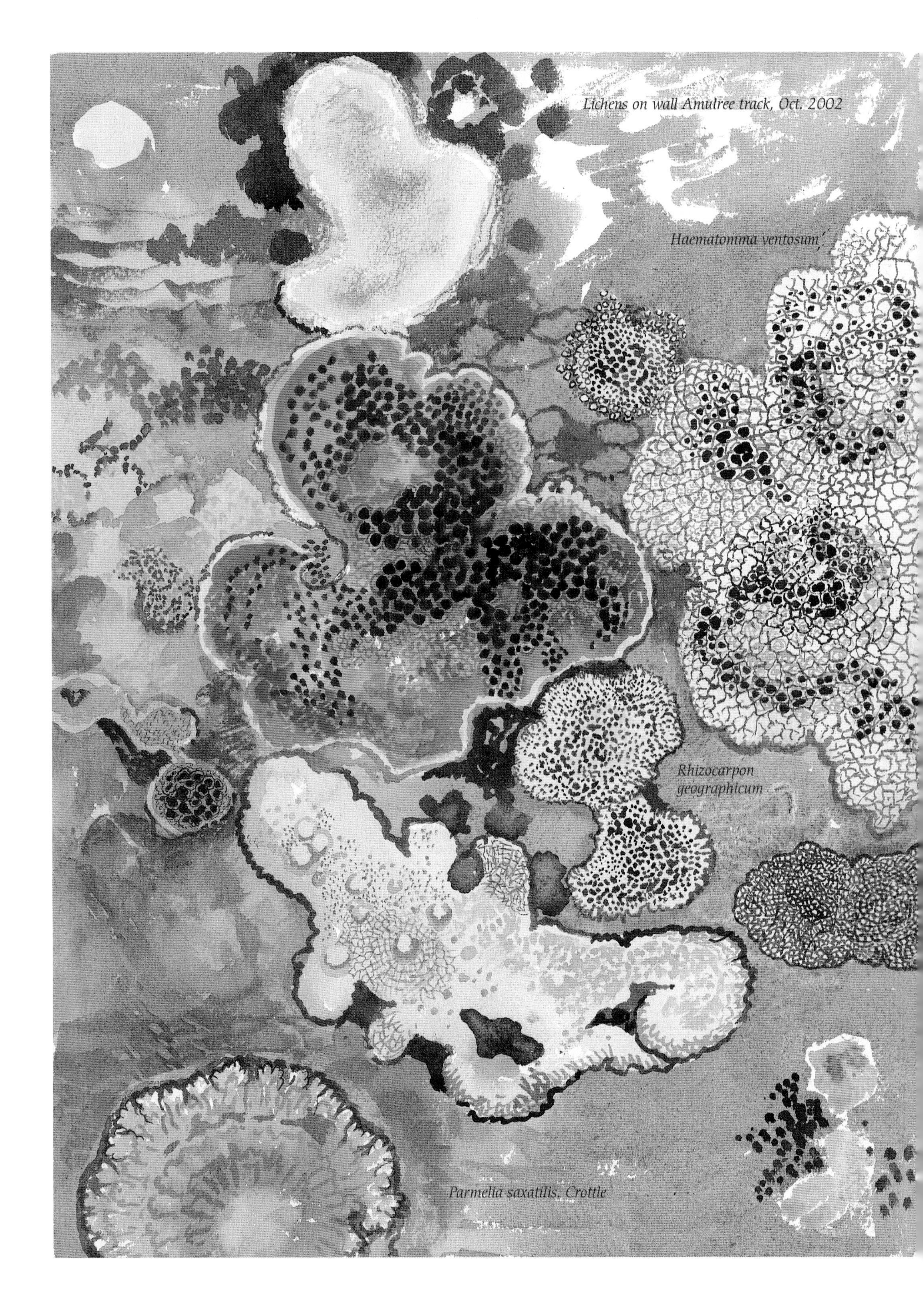
Lichens on wall Amulree track, Oct. 2002
Haematomma ventosum
Rhizocarpon
geographicum
Parmelia saxatilis, Crottle

*Ancient birch in The Hazel Wood,*
*Oct. '97*

With a hazel nut
Whisking tail
in irritation
Bouncing along top of wall
Memory sketches Sept. '97
NJG

*Red squirrel ♀*
*found killed on*
*Aberfeldy road April 2001*

*Sketches of Roe doe in The Hazels, May '88*

*Last vestiges of winter coat showing as grey tufts*

*Glen Lyon from Drummond Hill*

*Sketches of autumn Pine martens from memory after seeing film*

*Wild boar sows, Oct. '91*

*Mole ♂, found dead, Portbane field,
June 2000 (poisoned?)*

*A fox in The Hazels*

*Very quick sketches of half-grown fox cubs*

*The Lyon at Duneaves, Sept. '89*

## Autumn Glen Lyon

Snow-streaked mist-dimmed hillsides frown
Above steep-sliding valley sides,
Ochre dulled to bear-pelt brown
With bracken brakes of ox-blood red.
Below, tarry-bitter water twirls
Ice-white-fretted with hieroglyphic swirls
Around hollow-booming otter pools,
Along dipper-dabbled bars and shoals;
Overhung with fiery beech,
Dotted with yellow-spotted birch,
Glowering with autumnal larch.
And craggy mussels on the rocky river bed
Brood gleaming occidental pearls.

*Autumn salmon leaping*

# Autumn

Even in late August the first colours of autumn begin to appear in the trees; here a yellow spray in a lime, there a few crimson leaves on the bird cherries. In September there may suddenly appear a butter-yellow ash tree – yellow from head to foot. The colour in the bird cherries spreads like wine-stain and the rowan berries are turning red. But it is in October that the full glory of autumn is to be seen. Then the birches are veiled with the yellow spots of their leaves, almost like bunches of golden grapes; but the glossy foliage of aspens is perhaps the yellowest of all. Sword grass on the hills has turned gold-ochre and russet after frost, so that the land seems suddenly lit up against the grey sky and glows through a drizzle warming as a fire. The rowans, now with leaves turned crimson, yellow or orange, are thick with scarlet berries, and fat haws on the hawthorn taste of bread and apple, a feast laid on for the flocks of churring, chattering redwings and fieldfares that are now everywhere about the hills and fields. Larches on Drummond Hill are fiery orange once again, like frozen fountains of fire, and they begin to carpet the tracks with the brilliance of their needles as they fall. The loch itself is sometimes streaked with chains of these needles gathered into yellow lines by the wind.

*Aspen twig*

One day in late September a phrase of familiar music comes from above and you crane up at the blank grey sky. The sound comes and goes, and suddenly there is the first wavering skein of geese, tiny with height, the gabble of their voices sending an unaccountable, almost physical pang to your heart whilst it stirs your

*Greylag calling in flight*

*Greylags coming down*

blood with a kind of joyful expectation. Sometimes, when the geese are flying into a hard wind they tack in zig zags – a 'zig' of hard flying into the wind, and a 'zag' of gliding at a tangent to it – all in unison.

In October jackdaws investigate chimneys in Kenmore, a pair to each house. They take turns to get into the tops of the chimneys, looking thoughtfully down them. Sometimes they preen each other's necks or touch bills. I think they are staking claims on the pots for the next nesting season, but they also enjoy sitting on warm chimneys during the winter – although many houses no longer have open fires to warm them.

In fact, the autumn is a good time for bird watching as local birds become more conspicuous having finished breeding, and northern breeders such as some ducks, geese and whooper swans, are coming back. Others, of course, have already gone south for their winter holidays – such as the swallows, swifts and martins, flycatchers, cuckoos, warblers and osprey.

*Flight of ducks*

In October 1969 I saw a golden eagle cruising along the shoulder of Gunpowder Hill 'accompanied' by a peregrine falcon. At one time they almost collided but neither seemed to take any notice of the other, and they disappeared over a brow together. I wondered if the peregrine was hoping the eagle might panic a grouse or other bird that it could then catch itself. The peregrine was not mobbing the eagle, although they are often seen mobbing buzzards (and buzzards sometimes mob eagles).

One day in early November I watched a raven trying to feed on the wing. It carried a long object in its beak which it soon transferred to its feet. Every time it tried to peck at what it carried it lost altitude suddenly and had to flap upwards again. It kept transferring the object between its beak and its feet, and always when it tried to eat it lost altitude. In the end it gave up and followed other ravens into the distance, carrying the object in its bill.

Autumn, hardly less than the spring, is a time for breeding. When the River Lyon comes down in spate, dark and bitter-brown as stout, with patches of white foam swirling on its surface, salmon of the autumn run forge upstream, their torpedo shape honed by millions of years of such endeavour. A heavy splash in the River Tay or in the loch, shows where a salmon leapt as it heads towards the River Dochart to spawn.

On the tawny hill, stags force out their roars as the rut moves into full swing. You can see the steam of their breath leave the square caverns of their mouths at

*Leaping salmon*

each gutteral utterance. Black with peat-wallow, they seldom pause to feed but cover the ground with long strides, heads thrown back with antlers laid along their swollen, shaggy necks, as they hurry to challenge each other and to test hinds for their readiness to mate; or try unsuccessfully to head off a parcel of hinds which have no intention of staying with them – for hinds have minds of their own and know which stag they want to be with, if any.

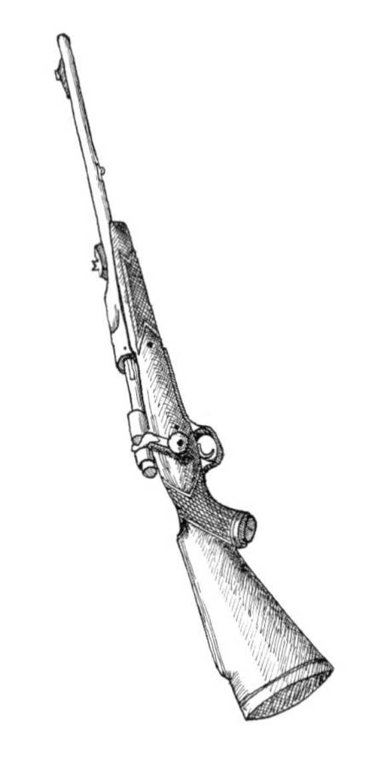

*458 Winchester magnum (model 70 super grade)*

In autumn selected stags are shot, and later, hinds are stalked. It is the old, infirm or injured, and the surplus that is taken, or should be. Wild venison (particularly of hinds) is a delicious, lean and healthy meat, unlike much domestic meat that is available from a supermarket. In the case of red deer, hunting by man is still necessary for they no longer have any other natural predator (in their case it was the wolf). Without predation, sickness and starvation would weed them out, but not before their habitat was overgrazed and overbrowsed.

In autumn, most wild animals, except stags, are laying in physical reserves for winter, and hedgehogs must stuff on slugs, snails, worms and beetles so that they may be fat enough to survive winter hibernation. Many hedgehogs and red squirrels are run over on the roads at this time and many young hedgehogs will die early in hibernation from being too light in weight. If help is extended to hedgehogs they must never be given milk, for it is very bad for them. Meaty, tinned dog food is better.

The fine mists of autumn fill spiders' webs with microscopic seed pearls of moisture so that they become opalescent saucers, each one tenanted by a small brown spider. This gossamer shows up how very many spiders there are, for their silvery mesh is everywhere.

*Red deer on skyline*

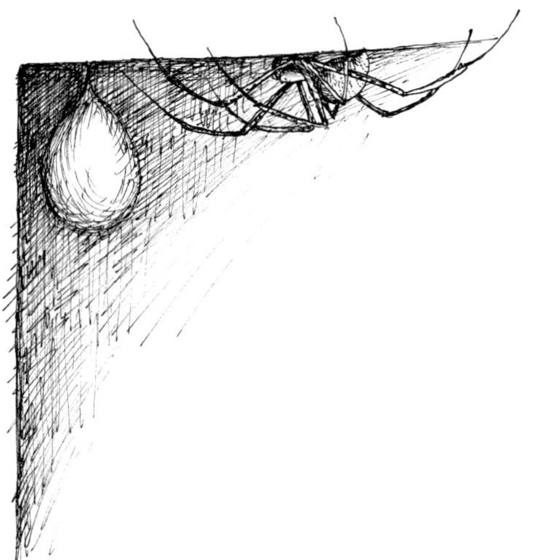

*Huge cellar spider with egg case (half life size)*

In the cellar under our house live some very large spiders (*Meta menardi*)that survive all winter in that dark, damp and cold haunt, living, I believe, upon woodlice. Beside them hang their strange, pearshaped silken egg-cases.

Some years oak trees are thickly spotted with yellow acorns and the hazels bear heavy crops of nuts. But strong autumnal winds sometimes blow all the nuts off the hazel bushes in a night or day.

Down on the stubble fields between the Lyon and Tay on one such windy autumn afternoon, the pigeons had difficulty making headway. A pheasant zoomed off downwind at break-neck speed, his tail whipping wildly this way and that. Mallards which got up off the Lyon stopped trying to fly upstream, turned, and at once were swept away. A thrush rising from the ground flapped hard but had to return to the same clump of grass. My husband Guy while out with the

*Mallards turning away from wind*

*Pheasant downwind*

*Guillemot on Loch Tay*

family in the boat on the loch could not get past the house, although he rowed on the spot for five minutes before having to give up. I went to watch a guillemot that had appeared a few days before in another gale. It was at the mouth of the River Tay in comparative shelter, while the wind still whistled over the loch and fanned spray under the bridge where I stood to watch the bird, hoping that it would feed. As I was about to leave, it disappeared. A minute later it was on the edge of some ruffled water, almost invisible. It sat up strongly to shake its small wings, so I was hopeful that it was able to feed itself successfully. Next day it had gone.

The first guillemot we ever saw on the loch was in June 1967. We have since seen guillemots there a number of times, and Douglas Hutchison of Bolfracks found one in the Square in Aberfeldy one autumn, which he launched on the River Tay near Wade's Bridge, where it seemed none the worse for its adventures in town.

Late autumn weather can be raw with the mists low and grey, day after day, chilled by new snow on the invisible hills; or rain may whip, wind-driven and gritting on the window panes. At this time many insects die off, such as worker wasps, bees and bumble-bees, while others such as their queens, and some butterflies, have begun to hibernate. Yet other insects will be active even in the winter, such as the shoals of dancing gnats one sees on milder days in windless places. One autumn morning I found a torpid rain-soaked bumble bee queen covered with large orange mites. After removing some of these, I fed the bee and put it in a box by the stove. Though it remained sleepy, it was obviously recovering. Next day, which was sunny, the bee flew out of the window, but upon my going outside too, it made a circuit of the garden and coming back, landed on my hand. As it showed no more desire to fly away I returned it to the box. Whenever I opened

*Kelso*

the lid the bee would climb onto my fingers – perhaps enjoying their warmth. In order to remove the rest of the mites it was necessary to take them by surprise, for they would hide around the bee's 'neck' or 'waist' where they were inaccessible. I fed the bee on honey or brown sugar and water. Next day it flew away and did not come back. (In 'helping' this bee, I had, of course, seriously incommoded the mites). Some weeks later Kelso would not settle for the night, making lugubrious sounds until I went downstairs to investigate. He was staring at a bird-box which we had washed out that day and put by the stove to dry. Inside was a bumble bee queen, and Kelso was nervous of the sleepy buzzes he had heard issuing from the box. We wondered if this could be 'my' bee come back to hibernate in its box, and finding the nest-box in its place, had 'thought' it just as good.

*Bedraggled queen bumble bee*

Wood mice come into the house at any time of year, but more often in autumn and winter. Sometimes when we enter the kitchen we see one, like a bun on stilts, its tiny feet pattering like a flurry of raindrops on the linoleum. I find mice among the most enchanting of animals, and would rather have holes in the carpets and dottles on the shelves than resort to killing them (although fire from chewed electric wires is a more worrying prospect – *does* it ever happen?) Mice

*Wood mouse*

*Baby wood mouse*

are great 'homers' and if removed from a house and released some way away, will often come straight back. There is a record of a marked wood mouse being released a mile from a house and being back there before the 'releaser' could get home. When I was at school the head mistress told me to get rid of the pet house mice I was then keeping there unofficially. Reluctantly I abandoned my biggest mouse, a beautiful 'champagne' female, about half a mile away in woodland; but she was soon back at my dormitory window having climbed up three storeys by the wisteria which covered that side of the house. This was the more remarkable as the mice had always previously been kept downstairs. She lived in a bird's nest in the creeper and I fed her for the rest of the term whenever she appeared, partly from a store we were collecting for a midnight feast on the last night before the holidays. My other, white, mouse went wild somewhere in the school and had a family of brown babies which I saw following their mother past the French windows during an English lesson.

A baby wild mouse I managed to rear not long ago (though it was still blind and nearly hairless when rescued by my daughter Laria) using a fine sable paint-brush as a 'teat', lived to be three years old – a reasonable age for a mouse (although I had two house mice that lived to be over four). It seemed incredible to have a satisfying two-way relationship with anything so small. But mice are wonderful little beings and if anyone doubts it, it can only be because they have not had the opportunity to know a mouse as I knew 'Mouti' (he was a white-bellied African climbing mouse, but I have no doubt that wood mice are as enchanting). Perhaps *character* and adaptability (intelligence) is strongly selected for in some heavily hunted animals such as mice, and this accounts for their surprisingly strong personalities. Rabbits I have kept also had strong characters when allowed freedom to develop them.

In the autumn, mice and voles make stores of food, and one September we watched the following vole 'acts' in the garden: rose petals taken, one at a time, into the hedge by a bank vole. Another vole (perhaps the same) cutting dandelion leaves and hiding them behind a drainpipe. Petals and green leaves would not last

*Bank vole 'smelling' aubretia flower*

long; but there was a third, more provident vole (or was it the same one yet again?) running up the trunk of a broom bush eight times, each time carrying down a fat pod which was stacked with others in a crevice of a wall. Eventually this vole was chased out of the bush by an irritated wren. We also saw a bank vole stand on its hind legs to pull an aubretia flower to its nose with one of its minute hands, as if enjoying the scent, but perhaps merely wondering whether to eat it. A bank vole which made a habit of eating food put out for the birds became so fat it could hardly move.

Runways of meadow voles in the grass and under moss have special alcoves used as latrines which contain their small droppings (in years of many voles these latrines are large and very well 'stocked'). Every so often an entrance 'proper' leads into the earth, or outside, from these covered ways. Bank voles and shrews find shelter in the many dry-stone walls characteristic of this country – walls which were introduced by the fourth Earl of Breadalbane in the early 19th century and many of which were built by prisoners of the Napoleonic wars. The walls also support interesting ferns, mosses and lichens, and snails with coloured shells of yellow and orange lined with fine brown spirals, that bank voles and thrushes enjoy eating. The tops of the walls are used as highways by red squirrels in the absence of the tree branches through which they prefer to travel. They use a wall along the lane to go up to The Hazels from Portbane wood to find and bury nuts there in autumn and to eat them in the winter months.

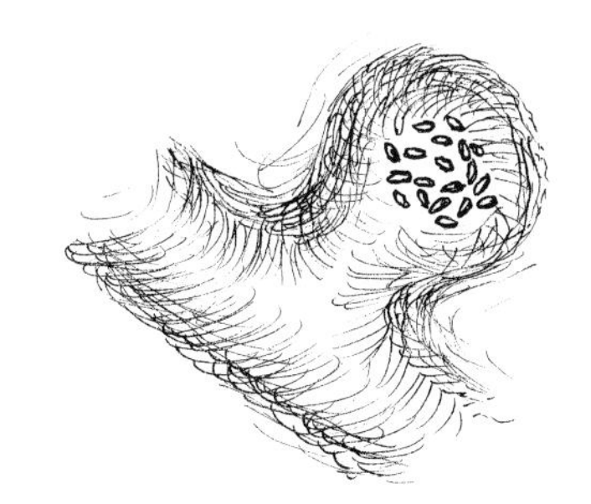

*Field-vole's 'lavatory' off runway*

There are funguses to be found throughout the year such as the strange, convoluted *Gyromitra esculenta* of pine woods in the spring, and the scarlet elf-cup; the chanterelles, pennybun and unpleasant stinkhorn of summer; but autumn is the season when most toadstools appear: delicate pedestals with flattened tops, smooth or shaggy, spotted or buff, mauve, russet or pink; poisonous, or edible. Tiny ribbed umbrellas and glossy pixies' caps in scarlet, pink, or butter-yellow,

*The Portbane lane in early spring, showing the squirrels' wall to the Hazels*

*Ancient juniper root*

appear in the grass, sometimes in fairy circles; or snow-white edible mushrooms with chocolate gills and the poisonous vermillion fly agoric glowing in the wet woods like lights. Wavy-edged flanges and frilly clumps sprout from dead wood and stumps, while brackets appear on the trees and puffballs in leaf litter. This is a wonderful area for toadstools and I have painted over fifty kinds already, with many many more still to do. Beatrix Potter used to paint fungi when she came to stay nearby.

*Marasmius rotula*

Although the country around Drummond Hill is sometimes wonderful for the seeing of wild life, there are times, of course, when you see very little, for Scottish wild life is very secretive. A landscape without it can be strangely depressing however beautiful it may be. Then it seems that the wild things exist only in spite of man. At other times you may see so much that it feels as if you are privileged with gifts, and this is often especially so in autumn. The following brief description from my notebook of a typical autumn walk perhaps illustrates how living things compliment and enliven the landscape.

*Clavaria cristata*

> 30th October 2001 ...... 'Straight to the First Forestry on Drummond Hill. Already the sun was low although it was only 3.30 pm. Walking fast along the level track until the end of the big trees, I could see right down the loch to Ben More, a murky-blue hump under flaming sunset clouds. The colours in the forest were stupendous. Even in the dusk with no sun to light them directly the beeches were like bonfires. Heard a green wood-pecker "yaffle" three times. Saw the ravens coming to roost, their wedge-tailed silhouettes briefly patterning the slit of sky above the track, and a flock of pink and black long-tailed tits mousing through twigs reminded me somehow of minuscule badger cubs, with their black and white-striped

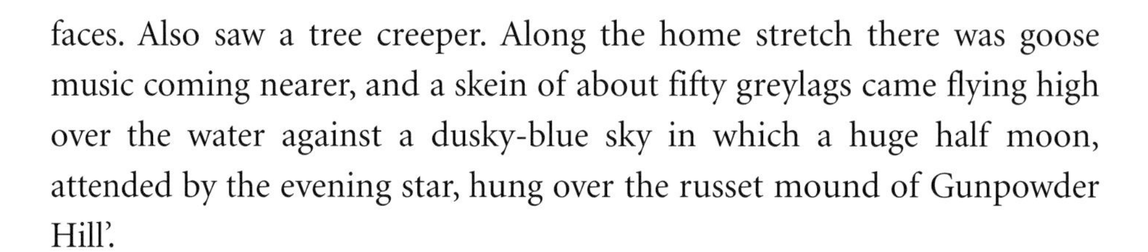
faces. Also saw a tree creeper. Along the home stretch there was goose music coming nearer, and a skein of about fifty greylags came flying high over the water against a dusky-blue sky in which a huge half moon, attended by the evening star, hung over the russet mound of Gunpowder Hill'.

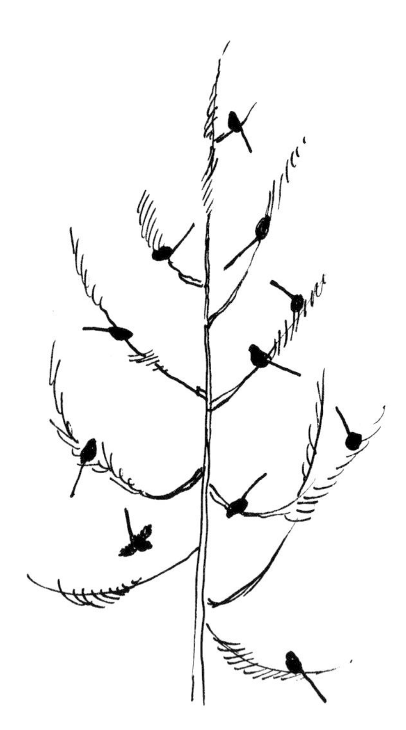
*Long-tailed tits*

Ben Lawers, at 3,984 feet is one of the highest mountains in Britain after the Ben Nevis area and the Cairngorms, and has a unique flora of rare alpine plants (owing to its height, climate and calcareous nature) which are described in books of their own.

Late one autumn an acquaintance and I decided to climb Ben Lawers. There was a foot of snow over the hills, in places drifted much deeper. The higher we climbed the larger the surrounding hills appeared and the smaller seemed the glens and lochs between them. Finally we were so high that all the other hills lay dazzling white below and we could see the whole fourteen miles of Loch Tay, narrow and sinuous, in places tooled like steel by an ice-cold breeze and the same blue as the sky – a great slit in the land through which it seemed one might fall. The glens were like the brown and green veins in a gigantic white leaf shaded with cobalt. How small those thawed areas where people lived seemed from there, and how great the area where people hardly ventured, and how unable to look after ourselves most of us would be there without our paraphernalia of survival. In the old days a Highlander needed only his plaid and a bag of oatmeal; the oatmeal he would eat raw with a little cold water; his plaid he would dip in a burn, wring out, and, wrapping himself in it, spend the night snug in a wind-proof ice cocoon. Yet when you are down in the valleys how much tamer and smaller the world and Scotland appear!

*Ptarmigans in winter plumage*

*The great Corrie of Ben Lawers, snow melting*

*Snow buntings*

Where snow had been blown off the hillside the crimsoned leaves of alpine lady's mantle showed in the ochre grass. A flock of small birds wafting high overhead with tinkling calls were probably snow buntings, though I could not be sure for they were silhouetted against the sky.

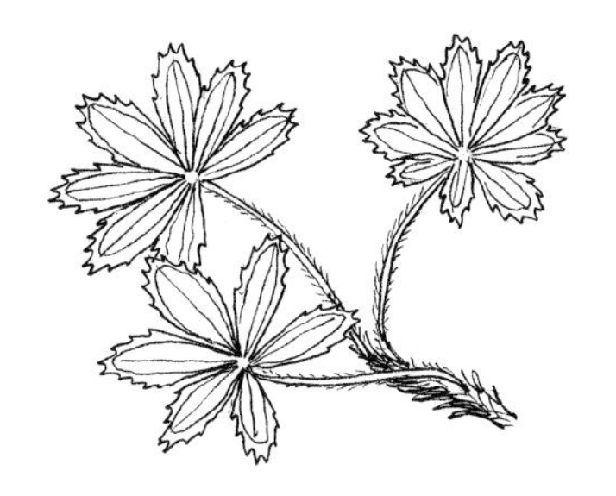

*Leaves of Alpine Lady's mantle*

At the top of the mountain mist was forming fast and the jagged black and white ridge following the curve of the great corrie, rising and falling with knife edges separating the summits, came and went eerily through it. On the bare, stony ground, kept free of snow up there by the wind, were clusters of sharp ice crystals like glittering flowers. We turned to go straight down for it was too dangerous to attempt to go any further in such conditions. But suddenly the mist closed around us and we found ourselves on a steep and ice-slippery slope that disappeared over a precipice. We turned back to try another way – the same thing happened. After a moment of secret panic, the third attempt brought us out into winter sunshine, and we began thankfully the long descent to the lochside road, and to hot buttered toast and tea at home.

*Ice crystals*

It seems to me that nature, dynamic, in a state of constant change as it is and of which we are an integral part, cannot be kept static, preserved in small reserves of one type or another, except as an emergency measure. But there are many encouraging signs that we are learning at last to work with 'it' instead of against 'it' (which is to work against ourselves). But if, after all, we cannot reverse the horrible trends in agriculture of the last 60 years and other shortcomings in our interrelationship with nature (which shortcomings go back a very long way) then we must surely change our name from 'Homo sapiens' to something more suitable and altogether less complimentary. But I believe that this beautiful place by Drummond Hill will benefit in future from gradual enlightenment.

*Old Scots pine*

*Sycamore leaves, Oct. '98*

Horse chestnut
(Aesculus hippocastanum)
Leaf from a tree by the
church at Kenmore,
which always turns red
in autumn
Horse chestnut from
Portbane wood
Oct. '98
NJG

*Fungi, Sept. '97*

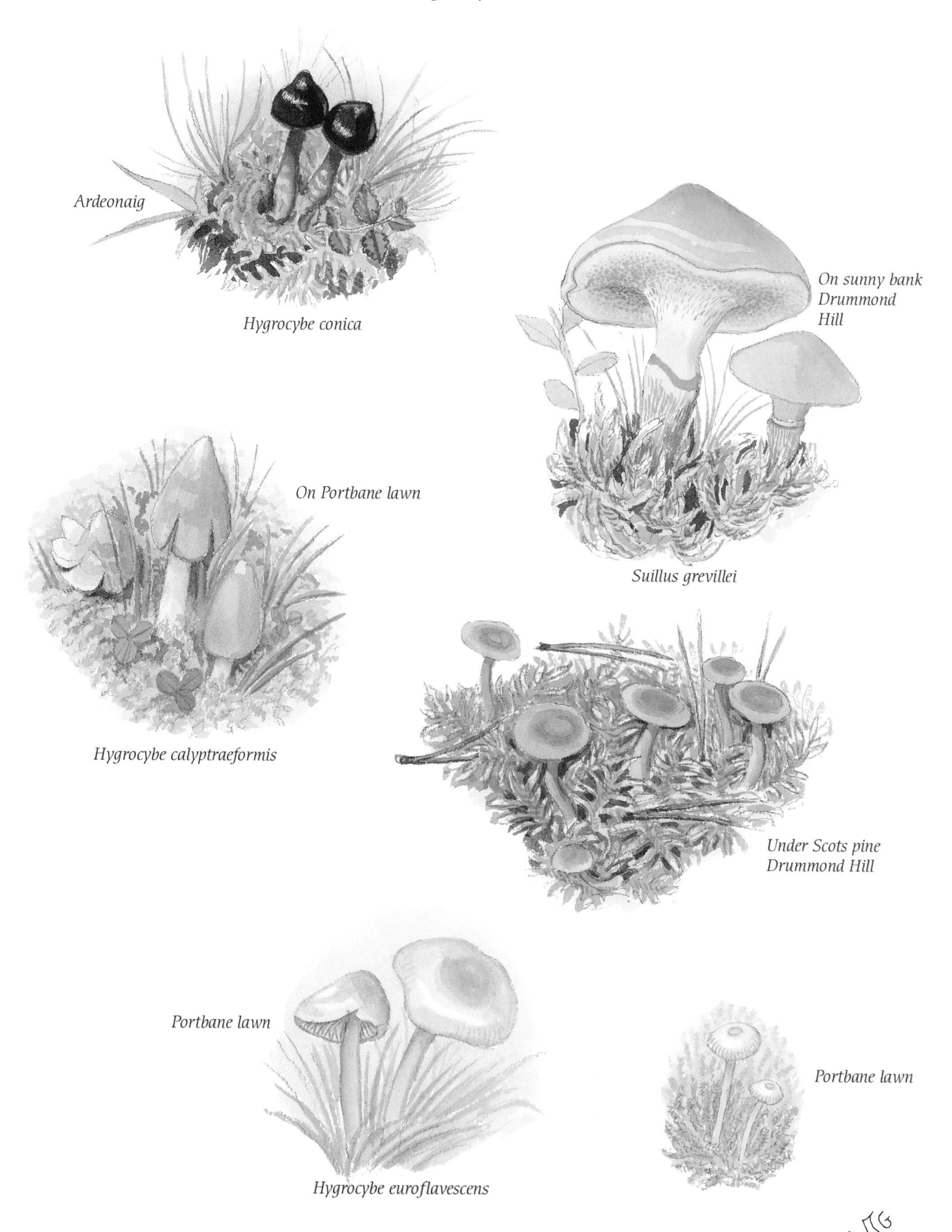

*Young hedgehog.*
*Portbane garden, Sept. 2002*

*Young hedgehog.*
*Portbane garden, Sept. 2002*

*Memory sketches of red squirrels, Nov. '98 (eating beech mast)*
*Drummond Hill*

*Fungi*

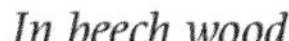

*In beech wood*

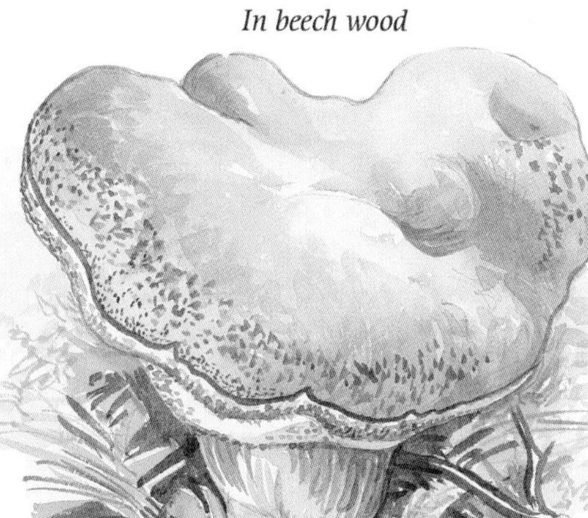

*Laccaria amethystina*
*at beech avenue, Taymouth*

*'Pennybun' under beech trees.*
*Cap very slimy and shiny in young specimens.*
*Underside pores as in boletus sp.*

*pale sulphur*
*yellow pores*

*'Pennybun' (Boletus edulis)*
*Under an oak beech avenue Taymouth*

*Cortinarius bolaris*
*Beech avenue Taymouth*

*Under beech trees, Taymouth castle*

Red deer hinds in Autumn
Waiting to come down into
The Hazels at dusk.
From my bedroom window
Aggression?
Not all red
deer have the
dark ring
round tail
area, Sept. '97
Mature hind
Young hind
A young hind in winter coat, Oct. '97
Showing the spread of hair around tail when
a deer is alarmed, Oct. '97

*Red deer stags during the rut*

*Hurrying to challenge a rival*

*A yellow stag*

*Working hard at his roaring*

*A beautiful head seen silhouetted one evening in The Hazels behind Portbane*

*A stag that has wallowed in peat bog*

*Evening light near Fortingall. Memory sketch Oct. '98*

*Geese above Gunpowder Hill from Drummond Hill. Memory sketch evening Oct. '98*

Laurel
Oct. '98
Elder berries
Oct. '97
Aug. 2002
Bird cherry
Sept. '97
Flowering currant
Sloes
Oct. '98
Blackberry
NJG

## Fungi

*Lactarius turpis*
*(Turfy bank, Curlew wood)*

*Cantharellus cibarius 'Chantarelle'*
*(beech avenue, Taymouth)*

*Nothopanus porrigens*
*(On dead stump, Curlew wood)*

*Amanita muscaria 'Fly Agaric'*
*(In beech avenue, Taymouth)*

*(Under birches, Curlew wood)*

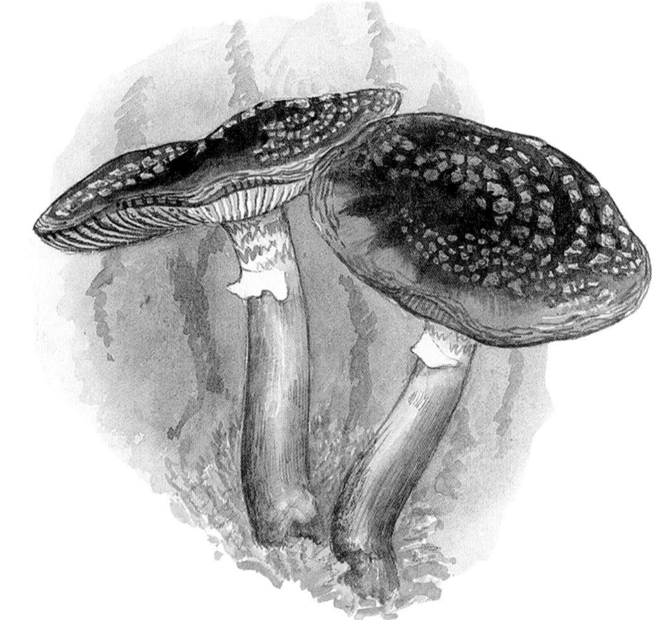

*Amanita rubescens 'The Blusher'*
*(Under ash tree, fields behind Portbane)*

*Cortinarius caninus*
*(beech avenue, Taymouth)*

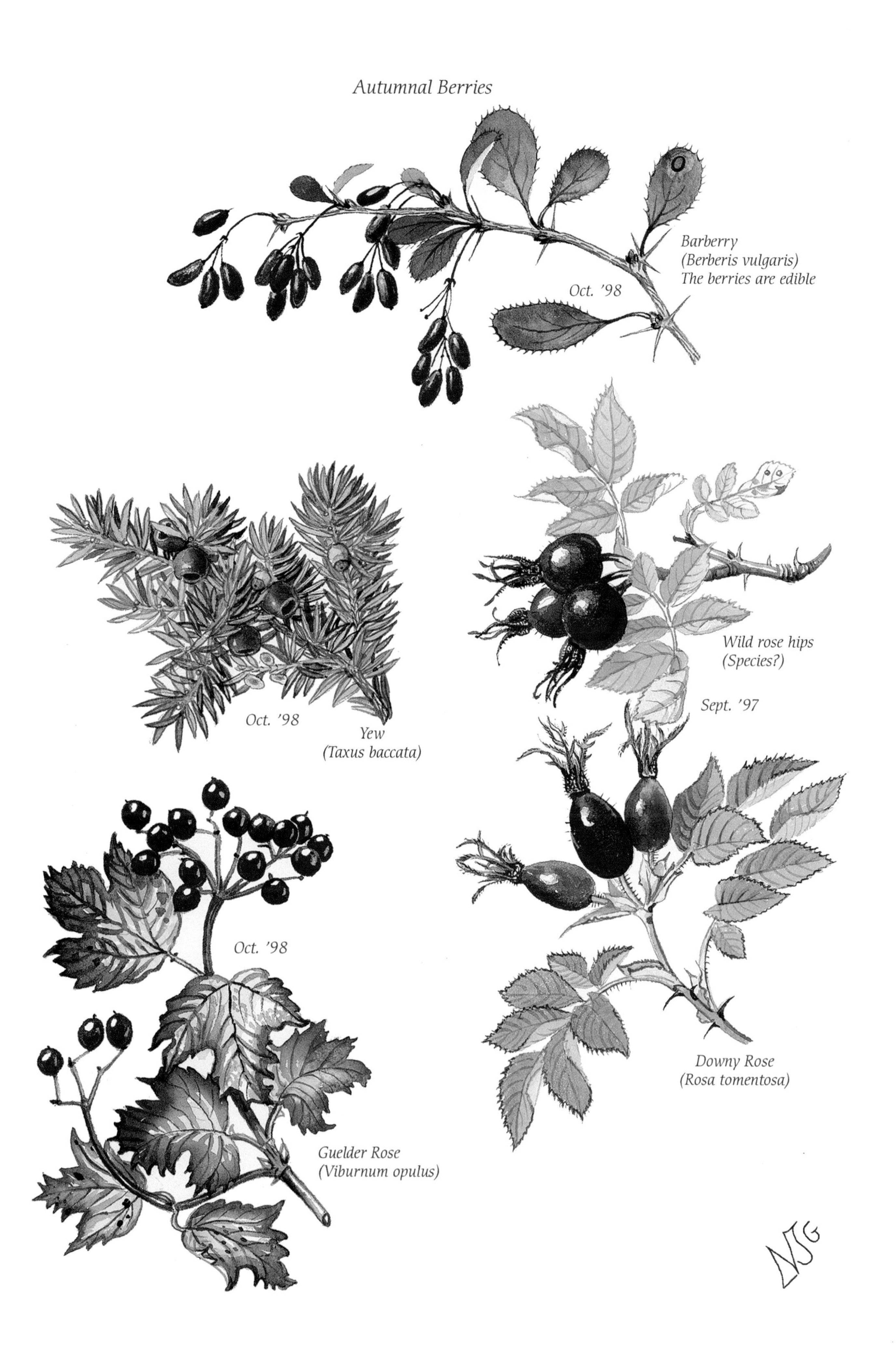
Autumnal Berries
Barberry
(Berberis vulgaris)
The berries are edible
Oct. '98
Wild rose hips
(Species?)
Sept. '97
Oct. '98
Yew
(Taxus baccata)
Oct. '98
Downy Rose
(Rosa tomentosa)
Guelder Rose
(Viburnum opulus)
NJG

*Larches. Drummond Hill, Oct. '97*

*Woodland Fungi in September*

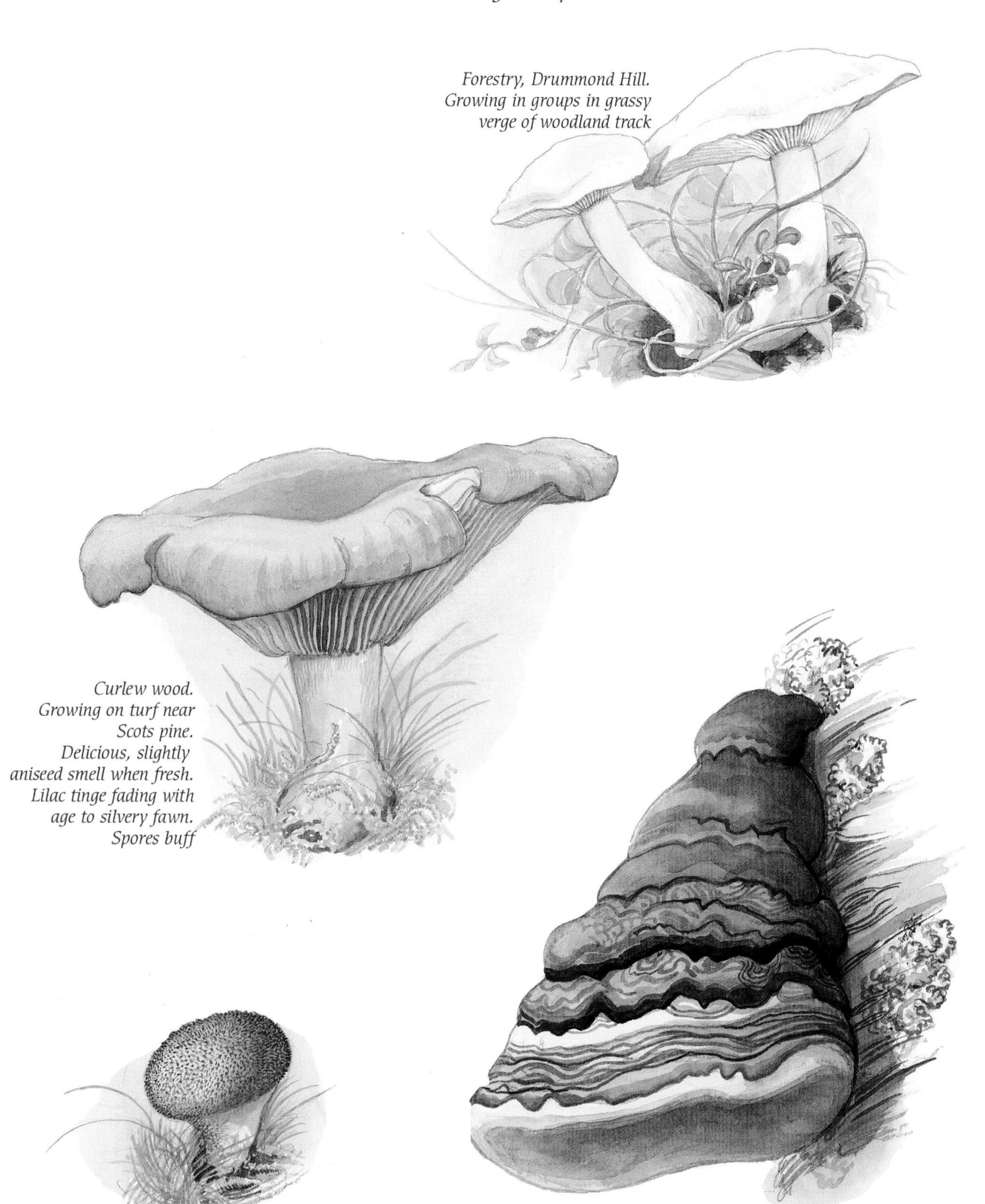

*Forestry, Drummond Hill.
Growing in groups in grassy
verge of woodland track*

*Curlew wood.
Growing on turf near
Scots pine.
Delicious, slightly
aniseed smell when fresh.
Lilac tinge fading with
age to silvery fawn.
Spores buff*

*Hard hooflike bracket fungus growing on dead birch*

*Curlew wood.
Growing under Scots pine*

*Memory sketch of red squirrel.*
*Drummond Hill. Oct. 2002*